Writing Reports

John Seely is a writer and editor of books about language and communication. He is an experienced teacher and has been a full-time author for many years. He is Series Editor of the *One Step Ahead* books, and author of *The Oxford Guide to Writing and Speaking* and *Everyday Grammar*.

D0167094

One Step Ahead ...

The *One Step Ahead* series is for all those who want and need to communicate more effectively in a range of real-life situations. Each title provides up-to-date practical guidance, tips, and the language tools to enhance your writing and speaking.

Series Editor: John Seely

Titles in the series

Editing and Revising Text	Jo Billingham
Essays and Dissertations	Chris Mounsey
Organizing and Participating in Meetings	Judith Leigh
Publicity, Newsletters, and Press Releases	Alison Baverstock
Punctuation	Robert Allen
Spelling	Robert Allen
Words	John Seely
Writing for the Internet	Jane Dorner
Writing Reports	John Seely

Acknowledgements

I should like to thank Alysoun Owen and Helen Cox at Oxford University Press for their help and support during the writing of this book.

Writing Reports

John Seely

Cartoons by Beatrice Baumgartner-Cohen

OXFORD
UNIVERSITY PRESS

OXFORD UNIVERSITY PRESS

Great Clarendon Street, Oxford OX2 6DP

Oxford University Press is a department of the University of Oxford.
It furthers the University's objective of excellence in research, scholarship,
and education by publishing worldwide in
Oxford New York
Auckland Bangkok Buenos Aires Cape Town Chennai
Dar es Salaam Delhi Hong Kong Istanbul Karachi Kolkata
Kuala Lumpur Madrid Melbourne Mexico City Mumbai Nairobi
São Paulo Shanghai Singapore Taipei Tokyo Toronto
with an associated company in Berlin

Oxford is a registered trade mark of Oxford University Press
in the UK and in certain other countries

Published in the United States
by Oxford University Press Inc., New York

British Library Cataloguing in Publication Data
Data available

Library of Congress Cataloging in Publication Data
Data available

ISBN 0-19-866283-1

10 9 8 7 6 5 4 3 2 1

Design and typesetting by David Seabourne
Printed in Spain by Bookprint S.L., Barcelona

Contents

Part A   **6**

1 Introduction   6

2 Different kinds of report   10

3 Defining the project   22

4 Research   35

5 Structure and planning   45

6 The process of writing   56

7 Editing the report   72

8 Presentation   82

Part B: Reference section   **90**

Part B Contents   90

Resources   116

Index   118

1 Introduction

CONTENTS

What is a report? **6**

Facts based on evidence **7**

Information that is checkable **8**

Presentation and style **8**

Audience **8**

Using this book **9**

What is a report?

We use the word 'report' in a variety of different ways in every-day life. Probably the first time in our lives that we come across it is at school: the end-of-term report, dreaded by teachers and students alike, although for different reasons. Radio and TV news programmes are full of reports and reporters. Indeed the commonest use of the word in everyday language is to mean a story in a newspaper or on TV: 'I saw a report about that in *The Independent*.'

> **Bloodbath at the Dome of the Rock**
>
> AT LEAST four Palestinians were killed and two wounded in Jerusalem yesterday after Israeli snipers opened fire with rifles on Palestinians battling with police in the grounds of the 7th-century Dome of the Rock.
>
> (The Independent, 30 September 2000)

Newspaper reports of this kind use ordinary language to tell a story, but sometimes reports are more like code than everyday speech. If, for example, you listen to the radio shipping forecast in Britain, you may hear the 'Reports from coastal stations':

> Channel Light Vessel Automatic:
> One thousand and four, west-south-west, seven, eleven miles.

This is specialist information for a specialist audience. Between the two extremes are a host of reports from businesses, government, independent think tanks, and myriad other organizations. For example:

> **Still Grey Suits at the TOP**
>
> Women in Publishing reports on the covert barriers within the publishing industry which prevent women reaching the board.
>
> The Bentinck Group

These examples might suggest that we use the word 'report' to cover texts that have little or nothing in common with each other. But that is not the case. All three have common features:

■ They set out a series of facts based on evidence of some kind.

■ The information they provide can usually be checked.

■ This information is set out in such a way as to be most useful to the reader. The reports have special rules or conventions covering how information is presented.

■ They are usually aimed at readers with a specific interest in the subject.

Facts based on evidence

Reports are factual evidence-based writing. The evidence may have been gathered at first hand by the writer, which is sometimes but not always the case with newspaper reports. Often it is the result of research into data provided by someone else. The data in the shipping report comes from the weather stations where the recording instruments are located. In the case of a campaigning report such as that by Women in Publishing, the data will have come from a variety of sources: interviews, press cuttings, and information taken from research done by academics and others.

Researching and recording evidence is covered in detail in Chapter 4.

Information that is checkable

The information in a report has to be reliable. Newspapers purport to publish true information; their reputations depend on being believed, and good reporters can normally vouch for their stories. They may refuse to reveal their sources of information, but these must be good and reliable. The same applies to official reports. These normally either contain the evidence upon which they are based or provide detailed references to their sources of information.

Presentation and style

See pages 49–50 in Chapter 5 for more about the structure of different types of report.

The whole purpose of a report is to communicate information and ideas effectively, so presentation is very important. Different types of report have different conventions. The shipping report presents just the bald data in a form and an order which its specialist listeners can understand and interpret. The most important information in a newspaper report is contained in the first two or three paragraphs, and more detailed or peripheral information follows later. This is so that busy readers can get the gist of the report without having to wade through hundreds or thousands of words. Business reports often begin with an 'executive summary' for the same reason.

Executive summaries are described on page 17.

Audience

There is more about audience on pages 22–6 of Chapter 3.

Reports are often prepared for a specialist audience. This is clearly the case with the shipping report and the publishing report quoted earlier. It allows the writer to assume that the audience understand a certain amount of information and are familiar with the style of presentation. On the other hand, the audience are to a greater or lesser degree 'experts', and may well be quite critical of the writing if they feel that it is not up to the expected standard. So there are advantages and disadvantages for the writer addressing a specialist audience.

Using this book

In this book we look at the kinds of report that many people are required to write in their everyday lives, whether as a part of their work or when, in their spare time, they are members of a voluntary organization. So it includes a range of typical business reports, but also the kinds of report, short or long, that might be required by a charity organization, a sports club, or a school board of governors.

The focus throughout the book is on clear thinking and careful writing. This is in contrast to many books on writing business reports, which offer a series of snappy 'tips' designed to make report writing 'easier'. Such an approach may seem superficially attractive, but it does not solve the main problem that anyone faces when they sit down to write a report: How do I collect and organise my material and then present it so that readers will read and understand it without difficulty? The faults of bad reports (and in my working life I have seen enough to write this with feeling!) are nearly always caused by sloppy thinking and bad writing. The application of clever tricks will never turn these into good reports, because the proper groundwork has just not been done.

The book is divided into two parts. Part A takes the reader through the stages of writing a report from the original idea, through to the finished product. Part B is a reference section. It contains a series of flowcharts and checklists to which you can refer when writing your own report. There are also extracts from good and bad reports with commentaries. Finally there is a list of selected resources and further reading.

I suggest that you read Part A in sequence. This will give you a clear idea of the book's main ideas and the reasoning behind it. When you come to write your next report, you can then use the flowcharts and checklists in Part B to guide your work. Here you will find cross-references to the relevant sections of Part A, so that you can check back to refresh your memory.

Good report writing!

Part A

Defining the report

Research

Structure and planning

Writing

Editing

Presentation

2 Different kinds of report

CONTENTS

Looking at reports 10

Brief formal report 11

Consumer research report 13

Pressure group report 15

Business committee report 17

To sum up ... 21

Looking at reports

As we have already seen, reports vary widely in length, scope, and approach. But when you sit down to write your report, there is one approach that is likely to be the most suitable for you. It's unlikely that anyone else will tell you what this is: you have to work it out for yourself. You will be in a much better position to do this if you have read and thought about a variety of different types of report, which is why this chapter is here. It will take some time to read, but studying these sample reports is a useful exercise and provides a solid foundation for the rest of the book. The chapter focuses on four reports; in each case there is a description of the report, with quotations, followed by a brief analysis. The reports are:

1 **Brief formal report**
   A report of a ruling by the Advertising Standards Authority.

2 **Consumer research report**
   An article from *Which?*, the magazine of the Consumers' Association, detailing the various remedies available for hair loss and its assessment of them.

3 **Pressure group report**
   A report from the British Helsinki Human Rights Group into sex trafficking between Moldova and Italy.

4 **Business committee report**
   The report of a working party set up by the directors of a not-for-profit company into remuneration and targets.

These are all real-life reports and the only changes that have been made are to number 4, which has been altered to remove references to the companies involved. Numbers 1 and 4 are printed in full in Section B.

Brief formal report

Reports do not have to be lengthy. This report from the Advertising Standards Authority (ASA) is only about 400 words long and consists of two main sections:

The report is printed in full on pages 109–10.

■ Complaint

■ Adjudication

Complaint

The 'Complaint' has two parts. At the beginning, about 100 words are devoted to describing the subject matter, a magazine advertisement. This was for a brand of golf ball and showed Tiger Woods and other well-known golfers. There is then a short account of the complaint:

> The complainant objected that the advertisement misleadingly implied that Tiger Woods used the advertised balls, whereas he used a modified version.

Adjudication

The 'Adjudication' section also falls into two parts. First is a 200-word summary of the advertiser's response to the complaint:

> The advertisers said the Tour Accuracy golf ball that was for sale and the Tour Accuracy golf ball used by Tiger Woods used the same ball technology ... They said that the only differences in the ball used by Tiger Woods were a slightly harder cover and slightly softer core, which were needed to accommodate his 125 mph swing speed ...

This section then gives the judgement of the ASA:

> The Authority considered that the advertisement implies that all four golfers used the advertised golf ball. It nevertheless concluded that most golfers would understand that professional golfers used modified equipment and that, because the advertised ball and the ball used by Tiger Woods were essentially the same, the advertisement was not misleading.

"Of course Tiger Woods uses a modified version"

Analysing the pattern

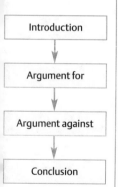

This report is, one assumes, the product of considerable correspondence and numerous phone calls and meetings, but it manages to pack everything into only 400 words. It does this by using simple, effective language in a well-established and straightforward structure:

■ brief introduction to the situation;

■ summary of the argument on one side (the complaint);

■ summary of the opposing argument (the response);

■ brief conclusion (the ASA's judgement).

This is a very common pattern.

Consumer research report

This report deals with two approaches to the problem of thinning hair in men: buying a product over the counter, and going to a specialist clinic. It falls into five main parts:

Introduction

This begins with a brief (200 words) account of why people go bald. There is then a consideration of whether it is possible to prevent hair loss:

> There is no known 'cure' for male-pattern baldness, in that you cannot make your hair grow back again naturally. According to our experts, lotions claiming to restore or prevent hair loss are unlikely to be effective. However, you could resort to surgery or wearing a hairpiece …
>
> Consumers' Association: Which? July 1999

Lotions

A section of just under 300 words explains what remedial lotions are likely to contain and how the products are intended to work.

Product profiles

Ten brief accounts, each following a similar pattern:

> **Foltene Research (solution) £23.95 for 100 ml**
> **Claims** 'Helps prevent hair loss'
> **Active ingredient** Tricosaccaride
> **Evidence** Research on people with male-pattern baldness showed an increase in the number of hairs from an average of 191 to 194 per cm^2 over 100 days.
> **Our experts' verdict** You wouldn't notice an increase of three hairs per cm^2.
>
> Consumers' Association: Which? July 1999

There is also an illustration of the product.

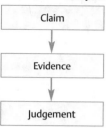

Claim

↓

Evidence

↓

Judgement

This:

is much more effective than this:

Each profile thus presents an argument in miniature:

■ This is what the product claims.

■ This is the evidence to support the claims.

■ This is our judgement.

The clinics

A section of about 900 words analyses a number of hair loss clinics, grouped by the type of treatment. Each consists of three elements:

■ the treatment(s) offered;

■ the prices charged;

■ a verdict on each.

Which? says

The report concludes with 150 words of general advice to readers on how useful the remedies and clinics are likely to be.

Analysing the pattern

This report is similar to that from the Advertising Standards Authority in that it presents an argument and then passes judgement on it. It is much longer, running to four sides of A4, and covers a lot more ground. It uses the layout on the page to help the reader. Each of the product profiles, for example, is marked off with a box and given space, so that you aren't overwhelmed by a dense mass of text. Because of this array of detail the report doesn't keep its judgements until the end, but places them against the particular product or service being assessed.

Pressure group report

Not all reports that deal with arguments work in the same way. Some prefer to build up a case point by point, quoting evidence to convince the reader. An example of this approach is a report by the British Helsinki Human Rights Group, 'Sex slaves: trafficking in human beings from Moldova to Italy'.

This report contains about 3,500 words of continuous prose, illustrated with a small number of facsimiles of advertisements and a photograph, and ending with a short bibliography. It follows a simple pattern.

Introduction

(About 15 per cent of the report.) This gives a historical background to the problems caused by the crisis in the former Yugoslavia and the mass movement of refugees and asylum seekers:

> ... in addition to the problem of large movements of people as refugees or migrants, a new and even more unpleasant phenomenon has accompanied NATO's military intervention: the dramatic increase of trafficking in human beings, most of which are women captured and forced into prostitution. Trafficking in women for the purposes of sexual slavery now forms part of a multi-million dollar business ...

The introduction goes on to show how Western intervention in the Balkans has exacerbated the problem by increasing the demand (among NATO forces and non-governmental organization workers) for prostitutes.

Moldova

The focus of the report is the fate of Moldovan women. This section of the report occupies about 25 per cent of the whole, and both details the local background and explains why the development of this trade in human beings has been so rapid.

The route through the Balkans to captivity

The report then follows the history and route of the unfortunate women caught up in this trade. This short section describes what happens to them in the Balkans.

Italy

Many of the women end up in Italy, and this section describes the situation there.

Sexual exploitation of children

A further section covers areas that do not fit into the main sections of the report. Some of the victims are young teenagers or even younger children. There is also a related trade in transplant organs.

Conclusion

The final 15 per cent of the report draws together the various strands and apportions blame. It comments critically on the money that is wasted by non-governmental agencies. It also points out that the policies adopted by the West in the former Yugoslavia are to blame. By posting large numbers of single young male soldiers in the region it has helped create the demand, and by failing to deal with the Mafia and related criminal organizations it has done nothing to solve the problem.

Analysing the pattern

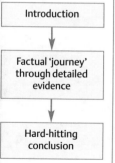

Introduction

↓

Factual 'journey' through detailed evidence

↓

Hard-hitting conclusion

A report of this kind does not follow one simple pattern. As was said earlier, it works by building up details to justify the claims made in the conclusion. Most of the material in the sections leading up to the Conclusion is factual and based on direct observation or newspaper, TV, and other reports. It begins with an Introduction which sets the scene. Then it follows the pattern of the criminal activities it is describing, beginning in Moldova, where the girls are taken, and then following them as they move from country to country. Thus the main part of the report follows a geographical and historical pattern. After a brief section devoted to related problems, we move from fact to opinion and criticism in the Conclusion. While the words used are strong, they are firmly supported by the mass of detail in the rest of the report and so stand up well.

Business committee report

This report was produced by a working party set up by the directors of a small company. The members were asked to investigate how the company's Chief Executive's appraisal should be carried out, his targets set, and his remuneration determined.

The report falls into three main parts:

- executive summary and recommendations;

- body of the report;

- appendices.

Executive summary and recommendations

An executive summary presents the report's findings simply and clearly for the busy reader.

On the first page there is a brief summary of the working party's findings:

> 1 Remuneration
>
> At present the remuneration of all staff (except the Chief Executive) is set by the Executive and is ultimately the responsibility of the Chief Executive. His remuneration is set by the Board. If these two processes get out of phase there is a danger that either the differential between the remuneration of the Chief Executive and his senior managers is seriously eroded, or the Chief Executive's freedom of action is severely limited. The Working Party came to the conclusion that there needed to be some formal arrangement to oversee all remuneration within the company and thus avoid that danger.

This introductory section concludes with the committee's recommendations to the directors:

> 1 The Board should establish a Remuneration and Appraisal Committee to advise Directors on appraisal and remuneration within the Company.

Body of the report

The body of the report is divided into five sections:

- membership;

- remit;

- evidence;

- remuneration;

- appraisal.

The first three are brief and outline the circumstances in which
the report was produced.

> **Remit**
>
> To investigate how senior staff salaries and targets are deter-
> mined at present and how performance is assessed ...
>
> **Evidence**
>
> The Working Party was advised by the Company's Chief
> Executive and Human Resources Manager and an external
> adviser, James Pearson of the recruitment company Executive
> Solutions. It also had documents on pay and appraisal from
> the Industrial Society, the City Bureau, and GDC.

The two main sections cover the topics that the working party
were asked to consider, remuneration and appraisal. Altogether
they contain about 800 words. Each section concludes with the
working party's recommendations, which are also printed at
the beginning of the report. Seeing them in context like this
allows the reader to grasp the process of reasoning by which
they were reached:

Remuneration

At present the setting of salaries and bonuses is the responsibility of the Chief Executive (except for his own remuneration, which is the responsibility of the Board). This has advantages and disadvantages. The Chief Executive knows what the Company can afford and he knows how well his staff are performing, so he is well placed to reward them both reasonably and fairly. On the other hand, if employees feel that they are being unfairly treated, the buck stops with him. There is also a large anomaly: if we are to maintain a reasonable differential between the salary of the Chief Executive and those of his senior managers their salaries need to be taken into account when determining his. Otherwise an imbalance can be set up. At the moment, however, this is not done.

The Working Party reviewed HomeAid salaries. Most of the figures we were using date from March 2001. At that point the salaries of senior managers seemed to be in line with those of comparable grades in comparable companies. Those of junior grades, however, did seem to be on the low side ... Although this is strictly speaking outside our remit, we recommend to the Executive that they take another look at this system to see whether it isn't possible to achieve something that is simpler and clearer.

In the recent past the Board has had no clear set of arrangements for advising on salary structure or for determining rationally the remuneration of the Chief Executive. The Working Party recommends that:-

The Board should establish a Remuneration and Appraisal Committee to advise Directors on appraisal and remuneration within the Company.

While the composition of such a Committee is for the Board to determine, the Working Party would suggest that it should have strong links with the Finance Sub-Committee.

The Chief Executive knows what the Company can afford

*Appendices are
a useful way of
recording
detailed data
that would
otherwise break
up the flow of
the narrative of
the report.*

Appendices

The report ends with three appendices (these are not printed in
Part B for reasons of space):

1   Present salary structure and pay scales;

2   Organization chart;

3   Pay scales at comparable companies.

These form part of the evidence that the working party considered in preparing its report. The body of the report does not
refer to them in detail (although this is often done) but it
makes generalizations based on them. They are printed in full
so readers of the report can check those generalizations for
themselves and make their own judgements based on the data.

To sum up ...

1 Reports vary widely in:
   - readership;
   - length;
   - detail;
   - structure.

2 It is possible to produce very short reports provided they have a structure that is easy to understand and use language effectively.

e.g. the brief formal report (pages 11–12)

3 Reports often present arguments. This can be done in different ways.

All four reports do this.

4 A common pattern is to state one point of view, then to state the opposing viewpoint. The report concludes by judging between the two.

e.g. the brief formal report (pages 11–12)

5 It is also possible to follow a similar pattern, but to repeat it several times within the report.

e.g. the consumer research report (pages 13–14)

6 Reports can also make a strong case for a particular point of view by building up the evidence for it step by step and then stating the case strongly in the conclusion.

e.g. the pressure group report (pages 15–16)

7 The structure of a report can be largely narrative (as in the ASA and Moldova reports) or more abstract, as in the business report.

3

Defining the project

CONTENTS

Key questions 22

Who? 22

Why? 27

What? 32

To sum up ... 34

Key questions

The first essential for writing a successful report is a clear definition of your project. To achieve this you need to answer three main questions:

■ Who?

■ Why?

■ What?

Who?

The question 'Who?' encompasses both the writer and the reader: who will read your report and what is your role as writer? It is a commonplace that the writer should always consider the reader when composing a text, but it is a rule that is often easier to state in theory than achieve in practice. You need to think of your reader in three different ways:

■ as a reader;

■ as an expert, or at least someone with a special interest in the subject;

■ as someone with whom you are in some kind of business or social relationship.

Reader as reader

It should be blindingly obvious that texts are written to be read, but it is surprising how often writers pay little or no attention to this elementary point. Look, for example, at this extract from a report:

> It is the Department's belief that having the Instant Access service up and running since early 1999 was an asset to Wansdyke plc; it indicates to the outside world that the Company has and is able to apply itself to changes in the marketplace.

The sentence is difficult to understand at first reading: the reader has to track back and work out what the writer *meant* to communicate. Such carelessness is less common, however, than a lack of consideration for the reader. In the following extract it is possible to understand what the writer means, but only at the cost of considerable patience and application:

> The total number of nights spent in officially registered accommodation establishments increased from 24.8 million in 1980 to 36.9 million in 1992. But it was not a steady rise because the rates dipped between 1986 and 1989 due to a slowdown in mass tourism throughout Europe in the late 1980s and rebounded in 1990–1991.
>
> European Union DG XXIII: Tourism in Europe

As a writer you need to consider how much time (and patience) your readers are prepared to give to your report. This will provide valuable insight not only into how you should write individual sentences (the style of your writing) but also into how you should organize your report (its structure). For example, a report written for use by business executives with heavy schedules will almost certainly begin with a brief summary of its main points, and detailed figure such as those in the extract above will appear in graphic form or in an appendix.

For more about writing, *see* Chapter 6.

For more about structure, *see* Chapter 5.

For more about charts, *see* pages 102–8 in Part B.

You may also need to consider the reading skills that your readers possess. Not all readers are of equal ability; if a report contains large numbers of lengthy and complex sentences with many polysyllabic words, then some readers will struggle to complete it. By contrast, if you are writing for a highly sophisticated and skilled readership you may well offend if you write in language suitable for a less advanced readership.

Reader as expert

Different readers bring different levels of knowledge to what they read. A skilful writer takes this into account when structuring a text. In the following text, for example, the writer has made a number of assumptions about the audience:

> Groundwater abstraction is essential to Three Valleys Water. The company, a subsidiary of Vivendi, abstracts 800Ml per day to supply three million customers, and 70% of its supplies come from groundwater.
>
> Sampling at the company's Bishops Rise boreholes in Hatfield last April revealed bromate concentrations of more than 200µg/l—20 times above the EC limit which takes effect in 2004. Three Valleys took one borehole out of service, and others supplying private customers were also taken out.
>
> According to Three Valleys, 'customers drinking from the supply would not have received elevated concentrations of the chemical owing to blending of the water from the borehole with water from other supplies'.
>
> Environmental Data Services Ltd: The Ends Report February 2001

This extract uses a number of technical terms which the readers are expect to be familiar with: 'groundwater abstraction' and 'bromate concentrations', for example. They are also expected to understand the abbreviations 'Ml' and 'µg/l'. Since the text is taken from a regular report published by Environmental Data Services Ltd, these are reasonable assumptions. Indeed, if the writer took time to explain all these terms, the target readers would feel frustrated and patronized.

So it is important to pitch the knowledge level of a report correctly. Like the consideration of readers as readers, this operates at the level of individual sentences, but also affects the overall structure of the report. (For example, do you need to keep explaining acronyms and technical terms, do you put them in a glossary, or do you expect readers to know them?)

It is a useful idea to include an 'acronym buster' at the end of your report.

Your relationship with your reader

When considering your readers' skills and knowledge, your aim is to communicate with them as effectively as possible. But you should also be seeking to establish some kind of rapport with them. The nature of that rapport varies widely, as is shown by these two brief extracts from reports:

> 1
>
> The English countryside is renowned for its rich diversity and cultural heritage, resulting from the interplay between natural processes and changing patterns of land use over the millennia since the first human settlers. This diversity …
>
> The Countryside Agency: The State of the Countryside 2001

Long sentences and impersonal expressions are typical of formal writing.

> 2
>
> The next day was nicer weather-wise, so consequently Geoff, Danny, Franziska and I decided to do a nice bimbly walk. We wandered north of the Barn, and after a daring stream crossing (it had been raining just a tad you see), we had a look at the limestone pavements, and then Sunbiggin Tarn …
>
> Cambridge University Hill Walking Club website

Words like 'bimbly' and 'a tad' are informal, as are expressions like 'you see'.

Extract 1 is fairly formal in tone, providing its information in a measured, neutral way. By contrast, Extract 2 is casual and rather flippant. This is in keeping with the kind of report each comes from: the first is taken from a report by the Countryside Agency, and its readers would expect to be informed but not be joked with. The second, on the other hand, is from the website of a university walking club, and readers would not expect their informer to take himself or herself too seriously. Once again, the relationship between writer and reader affects both the writing style and the structure of a report.

Do! imagine your reader reacting to **how** your report is written.

Don't! assume you can write in the same way for any audience and any situation.

Mixed readership

If a report is being prepared for a clearly defined readership, then it is possible to answer the question 'Who?' fairly precisely. Often, however, you will find yourself writing for a more heterogeneous readership. A good example of this is the reports on school inspections prepared in England by the Office for Standards in Education, or Ofsted. These are official reports formally addressed to the government, to the local education authority, and to the principal and governors of the school. So they are addressed to experts and need to be fairly formal in tone. On the other hand, these reports will also be read by the teachers at the school and by many of the parents. If they are too formal and 'expert' in their approach they will fail to communicate effectively. Some of the parents reading the report may themselves be slow readers. So the writers of such reports have to judge their tone and writing style with considerable care. For example:

> This is a highly effective school. Children under five receive a flying start to their education in the reception class and make great strides in their learning whilst there. Very good teaching continues in Key Stages 1 and 2 so that pupils continue to do well and leave the school with levels of attainment higher than average. The school is very well led and reflects on its own practice effectively, for example, recognizing and taking action on the standards of more able girls in mathematics. This high level of effectiveness is achieved at a cost per pupil that is broadly average, and consequently the school offers good value for money.
>
> Office for Standards in Education: Report on Aldingbourne Primary School 2000

Why?

The other main consideration apart from audience is the **purpose** of a report.

Think carefully about **WHY** you are writing the report— what do you want to achieve?

Information

Above all, reports have to inform. If they fail to provide relevant and accurate information, then there is little point in them. Information needs to be presented clearly and appropriately. Sometimes this is in the form of continuous prose:

> Pesticide use in agriculture in the UK declined from 40,768 tonnes of active ingredients in 1985–87 to 34,910 tonnes in 1995–97 (OECD 2001). MAFF (2000c) also reported a downward trend in Great Britain in active ingredients other than sulphuric acid used, from just under 32,000 tonnes in 1982 to about 22,000 tonnes in 1997.
>
> The Countryside Agency op. cit.

This information can, however, also be presented visually. You could show the information as a graph:

There is more about the visual presentation of information in Part B on pages 102–8.

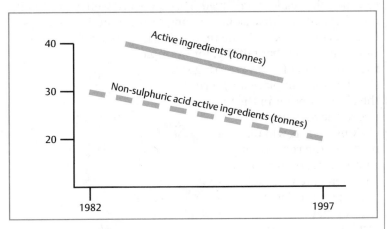

The same information could be presented graphically in a number of other ways.

| # Interpretation

A report is not just a bald recitation of facts; it also has to explain the information it contains. To do this it presents an **argument**, normally in continuous prose. This tells the reader how important individual pieces of information are and how they relate to each other:

> MAFF (2000c) also reported a downward trend in Great Britain in active ingredients other than sulphuric acid used from just under 32,000 tonnes in 1982 to about 22,000 tonnes in 1997. This reduction is partly explained by reductions in crop prices, and greater efficiency of pesticide use through improved practices and technology.
>
> The Countryside Agency op. cit.

After reading a report the reader should have a clear mental grasp of the essentials of the subject. To achieve this the writer has to give very careful thought to the structure of the report.

Detail—if in doubt, leave it out (or remove it to an appendix).

If the main argument contains too much detailed information it can become difficult or impossible to follow. A common practice is to place detailed information in one or more appendices to which the reader is referred. This can work well, provided it does not become wearisome moving forwards and backwards in a bulky document. If the report is to be published electronically—as an Acrobat pdf file, for example—then this kind of cross-referring is much simpler. You can place a hyperlink at the relevant point in the narrative of the document: clicking on this will take the reader to the related set of data. A 'return' hyperlink will then take you back to the point in the narrative you have just left.

Persuasion

It is only a short step from interpretation to persuasion. It is usually possible to interpret information in more than one way. Naturally you believe that your interpretation is the correct one, so you will want to 'sell' it to the reader.

> There is, however, no link between this appraisal and the system now established within the rest of the company. This is clearly illogical, since until the Chief Executive has his annual targets set he cannot realistically set those of his senior managers.
>
> Office for Standards in Education op. cit.

This is often the best way to write, although you also have a responsibility to indicate when there are two interpretations both of which have real merit—even if you then go on to explain why one of them is preferable. There is nothing more irritating than the kind of writing that constantly sits on the fence and refuses to take a clear line. Readers are left feeling that if they have to do all the decision-making they might as well have written the report themselves.

Do! express clearly where you stand.

Don't! sit on the fence.

Reports often have to make recommendations for action. This is another step on from interpretation. In an Ofsted school report, for example, a school will be told what it has to do in order to improve:

> This is a highly effective school with no areas of significant weakness. Nevertheless, the governors, head teacher, and staff should consider the following minor points in their future planning. They should:
>
> ● Devise a system of recording pupils' attainment so that rigorous short-term, specific, measurable, achievable targets can be set ...

Similarly, business reports often have to recommend which course of action is most suitable:

> The Remuneration and Appraisal Committee should be responsible for the Chief Executive's appraisal and target-setting. This process should take place in January and February of each year.

Reports
inform and recommend.

Proposals
sell ... sell ... sell.

This can lead some writers to view a report as a selling document: 'Write a good report on it so that we can sell the idea to the Board.' While it is true that many reports have a selling function, they differ from **proposals**, which are purely selling documents. In a proposal the factual element may be slight, or even at times non-existent. For example, a book proposal is a document in which an author describes a book that is not yet written. It outlines the book's contents and approach and possibly contains a sample of the writing style. As many authors and publishers know, the finished book is often quite different from the proposal!

A report, on the other hand, is based on evidence to which the writer(s) can point as established fact. This may form the springboard for recommendations, but without the facts these are weak if not useless.

Recording

A final purpose of reports, and one which can be overlooked, is to provide a record. Sometimes this function is explicit:

> The year since the publication of our last State of the Countryside report (Countryside Agency 2000) has been an eventful one for the countryside, and for some, especially in the farming community, one of great change and difficulty. The year also saw the publication in November 2000 of the Rural White Paper (DETR and MAFF, 2000). In the same month, the Countryside and Rights of Way Bill received Royal Assent. Countryside issues, such as genetically modified crops, hunting with dogs, farm animal welfare, and rural crime, continued to attract much media attention.
>
> The Countryside Agency op. cit.

Here the intention is clearly to provide a series of word pictures which will be stored and which can be compared (rather like family snapshots showing children growing up). Reports presented to a Board or governing body often have a similar value. Anyone who wants to know why a particular line of policy has been pursued will look back in files and read the reports which were prepared and adopted.

The annual report of a company illustrates a highly specialized version of this purpose. The financial part of a company report is a legal document, prepared according to strict accountancy guidelines. Around these the company may weave a web of words interpreting the figures, but the figures are always there and may be compared with those for past years.

"... another successful year ..."

This has important implications for the way in which you structure and write a report. The text should be as 'free-standing' as possible, without references and allusions that make sense at the time of writing but which may be confusing or obscure when read at a later date. The knowledge that your work will be read many years later by people whom you have never met and who have never heard of you can also have a sobering effect on your writing style!

| # What?

Your detailed answers to the questions 'Who?' and 'Why?' will provide most of the information you need to answer the question 'What?'—what kind of report am I going to write? Often, of course, a large part of the answer to that question is provided by your **commission**, or **remit**. A report is unlikely to be the result of individual inspiration. Normally the writer is asked or instructed to write it. The brief you are given should answer the questions we have been looking at so far in this chapter. If it does not, then you should request the information you need to help you answer them.

Before you begin work you should have a clear idea in your mind about the following:

- terms of reference;

- length;

- formality;

- status.

Terms of reference

If your report has been commissioned by a company or other organization, you should be given a clear definition of exactly what you are being asked to report on—what is included and (equally important) what is excluded.

> 1 To investigate how senior staff salaries and targets are determined at present and how performance is assessed.
>
> 2 To relate this process to the way in which the Chief Executive's salary and targets are determined and how his performance is assessed.
>
> 3 To take evidence from outside bodies ...

Try to get a clear statement of your remit—preferably in writing (especially if this is a paid assignment).

Length

It is essential to get a clear idea of how much you are expected to write. Generally speaking, the shorter the better. Busy people don't want to have to wade through pages of text to find the answer to a couple of simple questions. On the other hand, the organization you are working for may *require* a lot of detailed information. But it may not be easy to find out how long your report should be. Simply asking may produce only a rather vague answer, so you may have to focus instead on the amount of detail that is expected.

You should also find out exactly how much time you have to do your work. If possible, get this and other details in writing. That way there can be no argument over delivery.

Formality

Try to get a clear idea of how formal the report is intended to be. Ask who will read it and what will happen to it afterwards. (Organizations sometimes have a nasty habit of commissioning a report for one purpose and then using it for another one later on.) If your report is to be used by your immediate superior at work, for example, and will then be discarded, you can possibly afford to be fairly informal in the way you construct and express it. If, on the other hand, it is to be presented to a meeting of the Board, you will probably want to be more formal.

There is more about formality and tone on pages 69–71 of Chapter 6.

Status

Related to this question of formality is the status of your report. Some reports are obviously only temporary or interim, and will be superseded by another report in a few weeks or months. Others are clearly intended to put a lot of important information and ideas 'on the record' for the foreseeable future. This will affect both the way in which you research the report and the ways in which it is structured and written.

To sum up ...

1 Before beginning work on a report you ned to be clear about its audience, its purpose, and your commission or remit.

2 You should think about your readers' skills and knowledge of the subject matter.

3 You should also consider how formal your report needs to be.

4 Some reports are prepared for a very mixed readership, and this entails careful thought when developing a structure and when writing.

5 Reports can have a variety of purposes:
    ○ to provide information;
    ○ to interpret that information;
    ○ to persuade the readers to accept a particular interpretation;
    ○ to recommend a course of action;
    ○ to provide a written and/or electronic record for future reference.

6 The report's remit involves defining:
    ○ terms of reference;
    ○ length;
    ○ formality;
    ○ status.

Research

4

Working method

How you do your research will depend on the situation.

Solo

If you are working alone, then you have a considerable amount of freedom in planning and executing your research. That said, if you are a member of an organization you will almost certainly find that there is an element of teamwork in what you do, as you will be consulting colleagues as you proceed.

Work group

You may find that you are a member of a small team or work group within your organization. You will probably meet at the start of the project to arrange how the work is to be divided. After that you will probably develop a working method based on informal contacts, internal emails, phone calls, and so on. The key to success is clarity of planning and communication. It is easy for the patterns of responsibility to be left vague, only to find that at a late stage a key piece of work has not been done. In general it is best to assume that what is the responsibility of all becomes the responsibility of no one.

CONTENTS

Working method **35**

Sources of information **36**

Preparing to research **37**

Working with human informants **38**

Using printed resources **41**

Electronic information **42**

Recording and storing information **43**

To sum up … **44**

Committee or working party

Business and government reports are often produced in this way.

A different situation arises when you are a member of a committee that has been asked to produce a report. Probably much of your work will be done in a group as you hear evidence from different witnesses or advisers. Again, clarity is very important. It is essential to determine *from the outset* whose responsibility it is to record evidence and then to prepare the final report. It will also be necessary to allow time for drafts of the final report to be read and discussed by the committee. Ideally there should be full agreement on the whole report. If this proves impossible, then you may have to include a dissenting or minority statement as an appendix to the main report.

Sources of information

See Chapter 1

We have already seen that the essence of reports is that they are factual and based on evidence. So your first job as writer is to collect that evidence and then interpret it. Where you go on your search for information depends very much on the project, but most sources of information can be placed on this matrix:

Medium	In-house	Restricted	Publicly available
Human	Colleagues, friends	Contacts in other organizations	Consultants and other experts
Paper	Files Internal memos and reports	Research by academics, organizations, companies	Books, journals, magazines, newspapers
Electronic	Company/ organization intranet	Internet sites restricted to members only	Radio and TV Internet (free or subscription) CD-ROMs

Preparing to research

Before you even begin to consider which sources of information are likely to be of most use, you have to define very clearly
what you want to know. It's no good arranging to interview a
professional contact unless you have a list of questions you
want to ask them.

Make a list of the main topics you need to investigate. These
will serve as the headings for a list of questions. They may also
determine the main sections of your report when you come to
write it.

Impact of information technology on educational publishing

- State of readiness in schools for use of IT
  - provision of equipment;
  - training of teachers.

- Existing use of electronic product
  - CD-ROMs;
  - online material.

- Willingness to pay.

You can now use your headings as the basis for a detailed list
of questions:

How ready are the schools?

1 How many computers do they have?

2 What is the number of students per computer?

3 How accessible are the computers?
  - When are they available?
  - Where are they located?
  - How easy is it to use them in an unplanned way?

If you are interviewing informants, these questions will form the basis of the interview. If you are working with paper sources of information, you can use them as a checklist for 'interrogating' the book or other source. If you are researching online, you can use them as a starting point for working with search engines.

Working with human informants

Good interviews are usually the result of good preparation. Your basic list of questions is a good starting point, but you will probably need to adapt it for the particular person you are interviewing. Personal interviews are different from other sources of information because they are informal and—for the person interviewed—unprepared. If you are writing an article for a magazine, or even a memo for internal use in your organization, you usually give some thought to the fact that once it leaves your computer or printer you have no more control over it. So you make sure that the words on the page reflect accurately what you want to say. Speech isn't like that, and as a result people sometimes say in interviews things they wouldn't dream of committing to paper. This has advantages and disadvantages for the interviewer. It may mean that you get information and insights that are uncensored by any 'official' view. On the other hand you may be told things that, on further reflection, the speaker would amend or rephrase. If in doubt, you should check that a particular statement truly reflects the speaker's views and experience.

There is also the question of whether a statement, or a whole interview, is on or off the record. Since authenticity and accuracy are essential features of a good report, you must establish at the outset whether or not your informant is prepared to be quoted as the source of this information—and then stick to whatever is agreed. You have at your disposal a whole range of ways of attributing interview information: from the person's name and title through to a generalized description such as 'an informant at a large inner-city comprehensive school'.

Before you begin

Before the interview begins, you need to establish how you will record the information you are given. You may wish to use an audio recorder. This has the advantage that you capture everything that is said (including the tone of voice that is used). Its disadvantages are that it can be inhibiting for some people and that the resulting tapes take a long time to work through. Even if you do use a tape recorder it is advisable to make written notes as well. These give you a shorter and easier summary of the whole interview. They also mean you can record the spelling of names and the details of important factual information which may occasionally get lost in the recording.

Conducting the interview

At the beginning of the interview it is important to make your subject feel at ease. Take a few moments to talk about general matters: their role in the organization they work for, how long they have been there, what it is like to work for, and so on. When you begin to ask your 'real' questions remember to ask 'open' questions which demand a detailed answer, rather than 'closed' ones which can be answered with a simple 'yes' or 'no'. Questions that begin with question words ('who', 'what', 'when', 'where', 'why', and 'how') are usually open and productive. Another way of eliciting the information you need is to make requests, such as 'Tell me about …' or 'Could you explain …'

Don't be afraid of silence. It is often tempting to rush in with another question as soon as your subject has finished speaking. This is a common reaction, since in ordinary conversation we may find prolonged silences embarrassing. In an interview, however, silence can be useful. It gives the subject time to gather thoughts and add to what has already been said. Also, it can persuade a cautious subject to say more than they had originally intended. They see the silence opening up in front of them and feel that they have to fill it. What they then say can often prove to be the most valuable contribution.

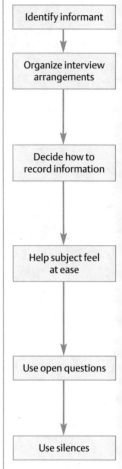

Identify informant

↓

Organize interview arrangements

↓

Decide how to record information

↓

Help subject feel at ease

↓

Use open questions

↓

Use silences

As the interview proceeds you will, of course, work through your list of questions, but don't stick rigidly to them. Be ready to ask supplementary, follow-up questions. You will often find that this kind of opportunism produces some of the most valuable information. At each stage try to establish the status of the information you are given. Is this information that is generally accepted as true, or are you being given a highly individualized 'take' on a situation? Both have their place, but you must know which is which.

Are you being given a highly individualized 'take' on a situation?

After the interview

At the end of the interview it is important to thank your subject for giving up their time and helping your research. Offer to send them a copy of the report when it is finished, and remember to tell them that, if the interview is on the record, their contribution will be acknowledged in it. It's also worth checking that you can contact them again if you think of further questions you would like to ask, or if there are matters that need clarification.

Write up the results of the interview as soon as possible afterwards. If you leave it too long, important details will become blurred in your mind. This is true even when you have tape recorded the interview: immediately afterwards you will have a much clearer idea of its structure and of the relative importance of different sections. Also, if you need to contact your subject for clarification it is much easier to do this in the immediate aftermath of the interview.

Using printed resources

Places to look for printed research materials include:

- your own company or organization;

- trade and other organizations;

- public and other reference libraries;

- bookshops.

Many organizations, including libraries and Internet book-shops, operate electronic catalogues. This means that you can search them in a variety of ways:

- author;

- title;

- keyword;

- ISBN (International Standard Book Number);

or by a combination of these.

The likelihood is that you will find too much information rather than being limited by not having enough. The problem is then one of sifting and selecting. It is important to be able to skim a document quickly to work out:

- whether it contains information that you need;

- the logic of the way in which it presents that information;

- how long it's going to take to collect information from it.

Many people find that it is best to sift through a mass of material in this way first before beginning to work in more detail on individual documents. This enables you to get a better overall picture. You may also find that something that looked relevant when you first skimmed it appears less useful when you have looked at fifteen or twenty similar documents.

| # Electronic information

An increasing amount of information is available in electronic form, either on CD-ROM or online. In fact some information is no longer available in print format at all. This has considerable advantages and a few disadvantages. Searching for the information you need is in many ways much easier. There is normally a search engine, which means you can enter key words and quickly get a list of all the occurrences of the word(s) you have entered. Documents in electronic format often have tables of contents and indexes in the form of a series of hyperlinks, so that clicking on an item takes you straight to the section of the document you want to refer to. In addition, you can usually cut and paste material you want to quote straight into your own word-processed document, saving time and reducing the number of inaccuracies that occur. Don't forget, however, that this material is normally copyright, and should not be copied and pasted, let alone published, without permission.

Advanced searches

Most search sites like Yahoo allow powerful 'advanced searches' in which you can combine keywords and use alternatives. Each site carries instructions on how to do this.

You may already know of existing sources of electronic information on disk or online. Equally, you can go to the Internet in search of new information. The big search engines such as Yahoo or Google can suggest unexpected and valuable new material. Inevitably you will be offered a lot of material that is either irrelevant or of doubtful value. But many large organizations and businesses offer a wealth of information, either free to those who sign up or on the basis of a regular subscription or one-off payments. If the reputation of the organization operating the website is good, then you know there will be no problems about the authenticity of the information.

As with printed information, it is essential to keep careful records of where the information came from and who published it. Again, you will need a well-thought-out storage system so that once you have acquired your information you can find it again when you need it. You may find it helpful to make a printout of all material gathered online, both for security and also as part of a print-only filing system.

Recording and storing information

You should establish at the outset a system for storing the information you collect and recording where it is and where it came from. As a minimum you need to record the following information for each piece of data you record:

- the title of the work;

- the author, if this information is available;

- the title of the paper, journal, or book from which it was taken;

- the publisher;

- the date of publication;

- the ISBN, ISSN, or other unique reference number that will identify it.

> Young People, Victimization and the Police
>
> Home Office Research Study 140
>
> HMSO 1995
>
> ISBN 0-11-341150-2

If you take time to do this as you go along—and do it for *everything* you read—you will save a lot of time later when you come to write your report.

Photocopying and making notes

When it comes to taking information from a document, you can photocopy it, you can use a scanner, or you can make notes. Photocopying is the quickest and easiest. You put the document in the machine, press the button, and you have the information you require ... or do you? You certainly have a facsimile of the page on which that information is presented. (Although you should, incidentally, make sure that you have the legal right to make such a copy.) But the very fact that photocopying is so easy can lead people to use it indiscriminately rather than making a careful selection of what they really need and then copying it. There is an argument that you get more—and more relevant—

information if you read a document carefully and make notes as you go. You may 'cover' fewer documents, but the quality of the information you collect will be higher. Of course, if you want to quote a large section of a text verbatim, then it is quicker and easier to photocopy it than to copy it all out by hand.

Scanning

Another piece of technology you can use for this purpose is a scanner. If you have Optical Character Recognition (OCR) software, such as Caere OmniPage, you can scan a piece of text and incorporate it into your word-processed document without having to retype it. (The warning above about the copyright position applies here too, of course.) The software is now very accurate, so that the amount of time taking up in checking for mistakes is correspondingly short, and you can save a lot of typing time.

To sum up ...

1 If you are working solo, different working methods will apply than if you are working as part of a work group or as a member of a committee.

2 There are a variety of types and sources of information available: human, paper, and electronic.

3 Before you begin your research you should work out in detail the information you are looking for.

4 Human informants can provide you with valuable data, but interviews require careful planning and execution.

5 Printed resources are widely available, which in turn entails disciplined use if you are not to be overwhelmed by information.

6 The Internet is increasingly a first port of call for researchers, but, again, there is a danger of information overload.

7 It is essential to have in place a good system for storing and retrieving the information you acquire.

Structure and planning

5

Planning

Unless a report is very short, you have to make a plan first. Reports are a fairly technical and certainly detailed type of writing where control is everything and 'inspiration' counts for little or nothing. So a suitably technical approach to writing is required. Making a plan may be boring, but it's efficient. For a short report you may be able to make a plan and carry it in your head, but in most cases you will be better off writing it down. In any situation where you are working with colleagues, this is essential. Otherwise, if you are unable to complete the project it will be very difficult for anyone to take over.

Types of writing

Before you make a plan you have to develop a clear idea of what type of organization your report requires. As we have already seen, reports can be very diverse in their content and approach, so there is no single right way of organizing one. To begin with, reports can contain three very different types of writing:

- narrative;

- exposition;

- argument.

CONTENTS

Planning **45**

Types of writing **45**

Typical structures for a report **49**

Simple report **50**

Two-part report with headings **50**

Multi-part report **50**

Detail versus simplicity **51**

The process of planning **52**

To sum up … **55**

Narrative

Reports often have to tell a story:

> In the last two years or so, there has been an exponential increase in the power of the Albanian Mafia in Italy. The man who for seven years was the head of the Italian anti-drug unit, Prefect Pietro Soggiu, submitted a well-documented report on this to the United Nations in 1998 ...

A typical narrative relates a sequence of events that happened over a period of time. So it has a fairly 'natural' organization: 'Begin at the beginning , and go on till you come to the end: then stop,' as the King told Alice. Sometimes this ordering is changed—for dramatic effect, for example—but the strong chronological basis of narrative always gives it a structure.

How a narrative is often organized

BEGINNING
Setting the scene and introducing the main elements of the report (the 'characters' of the 'story')

FIRST
What happened first

AND THEN
What happened next:
the next event(s) in
the sequence

and so on

CONCLUSION
How things ended
and the significance
of these events

Exposition

Exposition combines description and explanation: the writer sets a subject out in such a way that the reader can understand what it is and how it works:

> Integrated farming systems (IFS) aim to sustain agricultural production and maintain farm incomes, while safeguarding the environment and responding to consumer concerns about food quality issues ... Integrated farming combines pest management techniques, targeted inputs of fertilisers and pesticides, crop rotations ...

There isn't a 'story' to tell here. Instead, the writer takes a subject at a moment in time and provides an **analytical** approach. So a typical pattern is to begin with an overview and then look at separate sections one at a time, observing how they work and seeing how each contributes to the whole:

OVERVIEW
What it's all about

DETAIL 1
A detailed analysis
of one aspect of the
subject

DETAIL 2
A detailed analysis of
the next aspect of the
subject

and so on

CONCLUSION
Drawing the strands together
and showing the relative significance of each detailed section

Argument

In an argument the writer presents a point of view and gives the reasons for it:

> Organizations need to make the most of the skills and talents of all their staff to be fully effective in a competitive environment. Overt and covert discrimination against women means that skills are being wasted and potential thrown away.

A typical argument, therefore, states a proposition, looks at the pros and cons, and finishes with a conclusion.

How a typical argument is organized

PROPOSITION
What the whole report is about: the argument that will be put forward

PRO
The evidence and arguments in favour of the proposition

CONTRA
The evidence and arguments against the proposition

CONCLUSION
Weighing the two sides and explaining why the argument holds

Typical structures for a report

Sometimes you will find that one kind of writing is
dominant in your report. If this is the case, then the
type of structure that is normal for that type of
writing will probably be the most suitable
for your purposes. Some reports are
primarily narrative. You may, for example, have attended a conference over-
seas and been asked to report on it.

In such cases the sequence of events provides a useful way of
organizing the report as a whole. Other reports are largely
concerned with exposition or argument, and will tend to take
their main organization from these types of writing.

Many reports, however, contain a mixture of all three types of
writing. In these cases you have to base the shape of the report
on the nature of its content and purpose. But there are a
number of general principles.

Basic pattern

To begin with, there is a basic pattern common to the majority
of reports. It is grounded in the way in which you want readers
to approach your writing and to react when they have finished
reading. You want them to begin with confidence in you as a
writer and in themselves as readers. So you give them a brief
understanding of what the report will be about and possibly a
taste of what's interesting about it. Then you go through the
detail stage by stage. Because they have an idea of the whole
content, they are able to place each detailed section in relation
to the whole. Finally you sum up, reminding them of where
they have been and what they have learned. Even a report that
consists of only four paragraphs will follow this pattern.

Simple report

Short reports often follow this pattern with no more elaboration. One or more introductory paragraphs are followed by paragraphs in which the detail is spelled out. The report ends with one or more concluding paragraphs. For a report of no more than a couple of pages, this is perfectly satisfactory.

Two-part report with headings

Once you get beyond two pages or so, however, the reader begins to need more help. This can be provided in two ways.

1 **Begin with a separate summary**.
The first page of the report contains what is sometimes called an **executive** summary. This lists the main topics covered in the report and the conclusions reached. If there are recommendations for actions, these appear at the end of the summary, sometimes in bold type.

2 **Divide the body of the report into headed sections.**
This enables readers to find their way around more easily, and provides additional structure for the writer.

Multi-part report

At the other end of the scale of complexity, a report can be as long as a published book and be divided into many different sections. Such a report might contain the following:

■ title page;

■ table of contents;

■ overview/executive summary;

■ introduction;

■ body of the report divided into chapters;

■ appendices, including:
  ○ detailed data, diagrams, statistics, etc.;
  ○ list of sources of information;
  ○ bibliography.

Detail versus simplicity

5 Structure and planning

Many reports fall somewhere in between. They are more complex than the simple report and include some, but not all, of the features of the multi-part report listed above. As with many kinds of writing, the trick is to choose a structure that is as simple as possible but which enables you to include all the detail you want and make life as easy as possible for the reader.

This question of how you handle detail is very important. Since reports are factual, evidence-based writing, it is essential that you include sufficient relevant detail to support the explanation and argument you are presenting. On the other hand, if you include a mass of detail in the main body of the report you make life difficult for the reader. The more detail a piece of continuous prose contains, the easier it is for the reader to get bogged down and lose track of the main 'story'.

Your job as a writer is to sift through your evidence very carefully and to make judgements about which data absolutely have to appear in full and which can safely be summarized. The temptation is often to include something rather than exclude it—'just to be on the safe side'. But if you do this, you can almost guarantee that you will lose your readers' interest and attention.

But what if there is detailed information that just *has* to be included but which will clutter up the narrative of your report? There are two obvious solutions to this. While you keep the most important and telling details in the main text, other supporting detail is handled by:

■ judicious use of graphs and diagrams;

■ placing detail in an appendix, to which readers are referred. You may find, in a lengthy report, that you need more than one of these. The more material you place in appendices, the more careful you need to be in your use of cross-referencing.

The process of planning

You should by now have some idea of where your report stands on the scale of detail and complexity. You should have an idea of what type of structure is suitable. You are now ready to make a detailed plan. The following examples all come from the plan I originally made when writing the first draft of this chapter.

Block out the main sections

Begin by deciding what the main sections of the report should be. For this chapter the main sections were:

> A   Kinds of writing a report can contain.
>
> B   Is there a dominant type?
>
> C   Report basics
>
> D   Make a plan
>
> E   Flexibility

(As you can see, the plan was changed as I wrote.)

Work out sub-sections

Most if not all of the main sections will break down into more detailed sub-sections. So, for example:

> C   Report basics
>
> - Overview → detail → conclusion
> - Simple
> - Two-part
> - Multi-part

Each of these main sub-sections may then have more detailed parts, and you may want to add additional notes to remind yourself of things you wish to include:

C   Report basics

- Overview ⟶ detail ⟶ conclusion
- Simple (shorter, easier to use)
- Two-part
- Multi-part

  POSSIBLE PARTS:
  - contents
  - overview / executive summary
  - body of report (in chapters)
  - appendices

Outlining

The way of making planning notes is often called **outlining**. It is a feature of the larger word-processing packages such as Microsoft Word. In such programmes you enter your headings or topics and allocate each a level. Each level is distinguished by a different typeface or in some other way. You can then choose whether to show just the highest level, for the main topics:

Kinds of writing a report can contain

Is there a dominant type?

Report basics

Make a plan

Flexibility

include some intermediate levels:

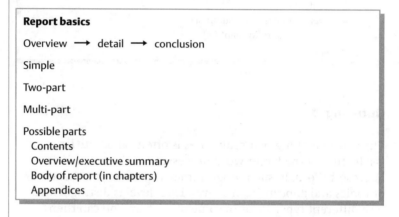

or show the whole outline:

You can also change the order of the headings. When you move
a heading of a particular level, you move all the subheadings
that belong to it. In such programes you can also switch
between the outlining mode and the normal text mode. This
means that when you are ready to begin writing the text, you
can use the outline you have made as your starting point. Some
people find this a very useful planning aid. Others (like me)
prefer an old-fashioned pencil and paper approach.

Flexibility

However you plan your report, the aim is to produce a plan that
is detailed enough to enable you to keep control of your writing,
yet flexible enough to allow you to make changes where necessary. It is rarely possible to follow the original plan exactly. New

ideas occur to you as you write; you realize that the balance between sections is wrong and needs adjusting; something that seemed very important at the time of planning is now clearly far less important than you originally thought. For these and many other reasons you will need to be able to make adjustments to the plan as you write. For this reason it is just as dangerous to *over*-plan as it is to make no plan at all. If you stick rigidly to a plan that is inflexible and over-detailed, you will produce a report that is dull and unreadable (and possibly wrong).

Always regard your plan as a rough rather than a straitjacket. Be prepared to be flexible.

To sum up ...

1 Reports can contain three different types of writing:
   ○ narrative;
   ○ exposition;
   ○ argument.

2 Narrative concerns events that happen over time. This gives it a simple, characteristic chronological structure.

3 Exposition describes and explains. Reports consisting mainly of exposition are often arranged according to different aspects of the subject matter.

4 Arguments have a two-sided structure that considers the evidence and reasons in support of and against a particular point of view.

5 Nearly all reports begin with a statement of the report's main contents. The structure after that depends on the length and detail of the report.

6 Shorter reports often have a two-part structure with headings. The first part is a summary of the report's contents, while the second contains the body of the report and the conclusion.

7 Longer reports also have these two parts but will have other preliminary material as well as (frequently) a series of appendices.

8 Detailed planning is usually necessary before you start writing. It is often helpful to do this using an outliner.

6 | The process of writing

CONTENTS

Drafting **56**

Drafting in progress **57**

Working at different
levels **61**

Workflow **62**

To sum up … **71**

Drafting

One of the reasons why some people find clear writing difficult
is that they expect writing to be a straightforward 'one-shot'
process, that flows uninterrupted from start to finish. But it
isn't. When you write anything longer than a few sentences,
you engage in a process that involves false starts, alterations,
crossings-out, and additions. You begin with something fairly
rough and then gradually shape it into the finished report. This
process is known as drafting.

Drafting versus editing

Drafting involves changing what has been written. For this
reason it is sometimes confused with **editing**. But there is a
difference. Drafting is the process of creating the text in the
first place. It is normally done by one person. (Even if the
whole report may be written by a number of different people,
the actual writing of a given section is usually done by an individual writer.) During drafting, as we have seen, the text may
be altered considerably—by the original author. When that
process is finished, the text can be edited: the structure and
expression are measured against the original intention, and
changes made to achieve greater accuracy, consistency, and
clarity. The editing may be done by the original author, but
often it is not, and, as we shall see in the chapter that follows,
it is better if it isn't.

What happens when you draft

Drafting is the process of moving ideas out of your head and onto the page. It is difficult to pin down *exactly* how this works, but it is clear that the preliminary stages of drafting sentences take place inside your head as you compose a sentence. Then, even as you are writing or keying in, you begin to alter the shape of the original sentence you thought of. When you have something on paper or on screen, you change individual words, the shape of the sentences, even the structure of a paragraph. As you do this, of course, you are not only introducing the new material, you are also destroying the old.

Not all new ideas, however, are better than those that came before. Sometimes you need to revert to an earlier word, phrase, or sentence strucure. You may go along one line of reasoning, think better of it and erase it to replace it with a second, only to change your mind and realize that the first was better. If you are writing with pen and paper, there is no problem—you can still see what you wrote earlier. But it can cause problems if, like many people, you work on a word-processor. With a computer the earlier words have disappeared for ever, so if you change your mind, you will have to re-compose the earlier version from memory. With a section that consists of a sentence or two that is not too difficult, but if it concerns something rather longer it may be impossible. It is a good idea, therefore, to save your text at different stages, giving each one a different file name, so that it is possible to revert to an earlier version.

Drafting in progress

At this stage it is probably helpful to have a look at an actual piece of drafting to see how it works. The example is taken from a real-life 'work in progress'. On the following three pages we can view it at three different stages to see how the writing changes.

First draft

Here we can see the writer thinking as he goes along. Most of the changes are to the wording of sentences, and there is one instance where he realizes he has missed something out and so inserts it at a later stage.

Writing is a process of refinement. We begin with a fairly rough version and

gradually, by a process of cutting, adding altering and so - we hope - improving, we

~~can be divided~~

work towards a finished product. The changes that we make ~~fall into two groups.~~

happen at different stages

· ~~those we make~~ as we go along

· ~~those we make~~ when we have finished the first draft.

placed in three categories

They can also be ~~categorised in a different way~~

· 'correcting' - putting right errors of spelling, grammar, and, to some extent,

punctuation

although punctuation is also a matter of style

· 'editing' - changing the way in which one or more sentences are written.

This can be to improve their style - make them sound better - or, if they do

not convey the meaning we intend, to clarify them.

changes'

· 'structural/ We may realise that, even if after careful planning, the shape of

the whole section is wrong and the ordering of the paragraphs, for example,

needs to be modified drastically. ~~Normally this~~

Normally this third kind of change should only be done when a first draft has been

completed. If you find yourself ~~chang~~ making major changes to the structure before

you finish the first draft, it suggests that your initial planning was seriously faulty.

Second draft

6 The process
of writing

Now the writer has keyed in the text, making more changes as
he does so. Then he has made further revisions on the printout.

Writing is a process of refinement. We begin with a fairly rough
version and gradually, by cutting, adding, re-ordering we work
towards a finished product. The changes that we make happen at
two different stages:

- as we go along,
- when we have completed the first and subsequent drafts.

~~Changes~~ es are of three main types:

The changes themselves

- **Editing:**
  changing the way in which one or more sentences are written, in
  order to clarify the meaning or improve the style.
- ~~Making structural changes~~:

  Altering the structure

  we may decide that even after the planning stage has been
  worked through, the shape of a whole section is wrong and the
  ordering of paragraphs need drastic modification. Normally this
  kind of change should only be done when a draft of the whole
  text has been completed. If you find yourself making major
  changes before you finish the first draft, it suggests that your
  initial planning was seriously faulty.
- **Proof-reading:**
  putting right errors of spelling and grammar. We may also
  amend punctuation, although this is only ~~partly~~ a matter of
  'correctness' ~~it is frequently~~ a question of style.

  *Sometimes
  and can often be*

Third draft

Looking over the whole text, the writer realizes that the ordering is slightly wrong. In the third draft this is corrected and a number of other changes are made to the expression.

Writing is a process of refinement. We begin with a fairly rough version and gradually, by cutting, adding, reordering, we work towards a finished product. The changes that can be made happen at two different stages:

● as you go along;

● when you have completed the first and subsequent drafts.

Changes are of three main types.

● **Changes to the structure**
You may decide that even after the planning stage has been worked through, the shape of the whole section is wrong and the ordering of paragraphs needs drastic modification. Normally this kind of change should only be done when a draft of the whole text has been completed. If you find yourself making major changes before you finish the first draft, then probably your initial planning was seriously faulty.

● **Revisions to the text**
The commonest type of revision is to change the way in which one or more sentences are written, in order to clarify the meaning or improve the style.

● **Corrections to grammar, punctuation, and spelling**
At some stage you have to put right errors of spelling and grammar. We may also amend punctuation, which is sometimes a matter of correctness and sometimes a question of style.

Working at different levels

When you draft and redraft, it may seem that it is a seamless process in which you are working on the text as a whole. In fact, however, you are working at a number of different levels and it is useful to be aware of these as you work. The chief of these levels are:

■ **Structure**
You examine the pattern of the whole draft to see whether it fulfils your original intentions. You also need to consider again the needs of your readership and the purposes for which you are writing. You check, too, to make sure that you have not moved away from your original remit. If you find a mismatch in any of these areas then you may have to make major changes to the structure of the whole draft.

■ **Paragraph**
The text as a whole is broken down into smaller units. Often a first draft is not divided into proper paragraphs, and you need to look at how this can be improved.

■ **Sentence**
At this level you are looking at the construction of individual sentences. This is a matter of *grammar*, *style*, and *readability*. Your sentences need to be grammatically acceptable, but that on its own is not enough. The style needs to be fluent and accessible, and your writing needs to be pitched at an appropriate level for your intended readership.

■ **Word**
At this, the lowest level of all, you are concerned with accuracy and tone. There are judgements to be made about how *technical* your language should be—and whether there is a danger that it will fall into jargon—and also about formality.

The bulk of the rest of this chapter looks at a recommended workflow in which each of these levels is considered in detail.

Workflow

There is a danger that the very necessary activity of redrafting will turn into endless and unproductive tinkering. The method I describe here is not the only one, but it is one that works. If you decide to adopt it, you will probably find that you need to adapt it to your own working style.

Writing the first draft

Begin by making sure that you have everything you need to hand: planning outline, copies of key documents, notes on interviews and on material you have read. Look again at the planning outline and get the key sections clear in your mind. Keep it beside your computer keyboard (or writing pad) as you write.

Then just write.

Write as quickly and as fluently as you can. Refer as little as possible to your papers. Resist the temptation to look back over what you have written. Just keep writing for as long as you can without interruption.

Don't worry if you feel that your expression may not be as elegant as you would wish, or that you may have mis-spelled words or missed punctuation points. All these things will be corrected later. The most important thing at this stage is to get your main ideas down on the page in as much detail as possible.

Proceed in this way until you have covered all the points in your planning outline and you have achieved a first draft. It will undoubtedly be fairly rough, but that is what redrafting is all about: shaping and polishing. If you are working on a computer, save this version as Version 1. If you are working on paper, make a copy of the original and do the following stages on the copy.

Revising the structure

Structure concerns the whole text and the way it is shaped. You should have done the basic work on structure at the planning stage, so when you look back at what you have written there are two questions to ask about your writing:

■ Does it fulfil my original plan?

■ Now that I've written it, do I still think it's the best possible plan?

If the answer to either of these questions is 'No', you have some reshaping to do.

Read what you have written, looking at the overall shape and impact. Check it against the planning outline and against the key documents you have been referring to. Look to see whether you need to make:

■ cuts;

■ additions;

■ changes to the ordering.

At this stage most people find it easier to work on paper rather than on screen. You can use highlighters and coloured pens to mark up your copy to show where cuts and additions need to be made and where sections should be moved around. If the changes to the ordering are substantial, you may even like to cut the printout up and stick it together again in the correct order.

This is the point at which to carry out the changes you have decided are necessary. Return to your computer; open Version 1 and save it as Version 2 before starting work. Or, if you are still working on paper, make a fresh copy of the original, cut it up as necessary and stick it together again, adding new material in the correct places.

You should now have a document that is in the correct shape; it shouldn't be necessary to make any further structural changes.

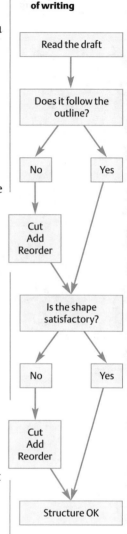

Revising paragraphing

Any text that is longer than a few sentences needs to be divided into paragraphs. Paragraphing has two main purposes:

■ It helps the reader by breaking the text into short sections on the page, thus making it easier to read and to find particular information.

■ It helps both reader and writer by giving the text a clearer shape.

The pattern of a paragraph

There are two essential sentences in any paragraph:

■ **lead sentence**
This is usually either the first or the second sentence in the paragraph. It has two purposes:
  ○ to indicate what the paragraph is about (the lead sentence should always do this);
  ○ to provide a link back to the preceding paragraph (it often does this, but not always).

■ **concluding sentence**
This is usually either the last or the last but one sentence in the paragraph. It has two purposes:
  ○ to wind up the argument contained in the paragraph (the concluding sentence should always do this);
  ○ to provide a link forward to the following paragraph (it often does this, but not always).

Between these two sentences comes the **body of the para-graph**. This consists of a number of sentences which develop the 'argument' of the paragraph, providing information and ideas that follow on smoothly and coherently from the lead sentence.

In the example opposite, these parts are marked and captioned.

A colliery sends to the surface more waste than coal, and a mining village has to learn to live with it. It must be put somewhere or the mine would close, and it's too expensive to carry it far. So the tips grow everywhere, straddling the hillsides, nudging the houses like black-furred beasts. Almost everyone, from time to time, has seen danger in them, but mostly they are endured as a fact of life.

lead sentence

concluding sentence

On the mountain above Aberfan there were seven such tips. The evening sun sank early behind them. To some of the younger generation they had always been there, as though dumped by the hand of God. They could be seen from the school windows, immediately below them, rising like black pyramids in the western sky. But they were not as solid as they looked; it was known that several had moved in the past, inching ominously down the mountain.

lead sentence ('seven such tips' ties this new paragraph to the content of the previous one.)

concluding sentence —it refers back to the content of this paragraph and forward to the next

What was not known however was that the newest tip, number 7, was a killer with a rotten heart. It had been begun in Easter 1958, and was built on a mountain spring …

Laurie Lee; I Can't Stay Long (André Deutsch, 1975)

lead sentence ('What was not known' links in neatly with concluding sentence of previous paragraph.)

Go through your first draft, checking that there is a clear paragraph structure along these lines. Make sure that your text is:

■ **Clear**
Does it say *exactly* what you intend, in a way that is as easy as possible for the reader?

■ **Concise**
Are there unnecessary words, phrases, or even whole sentences that can be removed without significant loss?

■ **Coherent**
Does it hold together so that the progress from one point to the next is logical and seems inevitable?

Revising sentence structure

The same three principles of clarity, conciseness, and coherence should also guide you as you revise your sentences. But they are more difficult to apply at this level than at the paragraph level. It would take a whole book to cover the topic adequately. It is, however, possible to suggest a few guidelines.

Sentence length

In general you should try to avoid long sentences. Occasionally you may need to express a thought of such complexity that you cannot avoid writing a long sentence. But such sentences should be the exception rather than the rule. In this chapter so far, excluding titles and lists, the average sentence length is just over seventeen words. That is possibly a little on the long side, and you should certainly aim to keep at or below an average of seventeen words.

Sentence complexity

Shorter sentences are certainly easier to read than long sentences. But it isn't just a question of length. Some sentences that are not particularly long may be difficult to understand if they have a complex structure. You can see this by comparing these two sentences:

Sentence 1
Shorter sentences are certainly easier to read than long sentences, but it isn't just a question of length and some sentences that are not particularly long may be difficult to understand if they have a complex structure.

Sentence 2
While length may important, although shorter sentences are certainly easier to read than long sentences, it isn't just a question of length but also of complexity, since some sentences that are not particularly long may be difficult to understand if they have a complex structure.

Sentence 2 is only eight words longer than Sentence 1, but its complexity makes it much harder work for the reader. If you find yourself writing sentences of this kind, try to 'unpack' them into a series of shorter sentences:

Shorter sentences are certainly easier to read than long sentences.	+	But it isn't just a question of length.	+	Some sentences that are not particularly long may be difficult to understand if they have a complex structure.

Thinking about the subject

If a sentence makes a statement, the subject usually comes at or near the beginning. It is usually a noun, a pronoun, or a noun phrase, a group of words built up on a noun. In the sentences that follow, the subject is in bold type:

Siobhan has just been promoted. (noun)

She heard about it yesterday. (pronoun)

Her line manager gave her the good news. (noun phrase)

The purpose of the subject is to kick-start the sentence by telling what it is going to be about. If it doesn't tell us what the sentence is about, then it points us to part of the text that does. (So 'She' in the second sentence tells us that the sentence is about Siobhan.)

There are two ways in which problems can be caused by the sentence subject. If you use a personal pronoun ('I', 'you', 'we', 'he', 'she', 'it', 'they'), it may not be clear who or what you are referring to, as in these sentences:

Edward phoned David to tell him that the meeting was running late and he would be delayed. He suggested they met the next day.

That last 'he' is ambiguous: who suggested this, Edward, or David? To avoid this problem, repeat the name.

Another common problem with sentence subjects happens when they get too long, as in this sentence:

> **The previous Managing Director, Sir Marcus Riley, a man of enormous experience both in electrical engineering and in product development, as well as being a skilled negotiator with an excellent head for figures**, has, unfortunately, left the company.

By the time readers have got to the main part of the sentence ('has left the company') they have lost all sense of what it is about. The subject of this sentence (in bold) is thirty-three words long—and it doesn't need to be. If you want to give the reader all that extra information about Sir Marcus, put it in a separate sentence:

> The previous Managing Director, Sir Marcus Riley has, unfortunately, left the company. He was a man of enormous experience both in electrical engineering and in product development. He was also a skilled negotiator with an excellent head for figures.

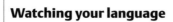

Watching your language

Finally we come to words, the individual components from which your sentences are constructed. There are three areas you need to think about particularly, when redrafting:

- tone;

- accuracy;

- jargon.

Tone

By tone we mean the manner in which you address your reader. Some reports are formal in tone:

> Carbon monoxide is a gas produced in the process of combustion, be it in a motor car engine, domestic heating, a cigarette, or a forest fire. Of all the pollutant gases, it is one of the most dangerous, since it can and does cause death.

Others are decidedly informal:

> The next day was nicer weather-wise, so consequently Geoff, Danny, Franziska and I decided to do a nice bimbly walk. We wandered north of the Barn, and after a daring stream crossing (it had been raining just a tad you see), we had a look at the limestone pavements ...

You should think carefully about the people who will be reading your report. This includes not only those to whom it is immediately addressed, who will read it when you publish it or send it to them, but also those who may read it much later. If you are in any doubt you should err on the side of caution and make your writing tone formal, or at least neutral, rather than informal or chatty. One way of checking on this is to try out the whole report, or sections of it, on one or more readers whose judgement you trust.

Accuracy

Since reports are documents that communicate information and ideas about that information, they must be expressed accurately. This means that you have to scrutinize very carefully the words you use. English is a language which offers us an enormous vocabulary, so there is almost always a choice of words available to us. Even a simple sentence like this:

> The police officer arrested the criminal.

can be expressed in many different ways:

> The constable apprehended the lawbreaker.
> The copper nicked the villain.

and so on.

From this flow two simple pieces of advice:

- There is almost always a choice of words.

- There is usually a right (or best) choice.

Most of the time you will have the words you need right inside your head, and simply need to pause for a moment to think about which to use. But nobody can do that all the time. We all need help with words from time to time. So it is always good practice to have a good dictionary in book or computer form and a good printed thesaurus (the computer versions are generally less satisfactory).

Jargon

Reports often deal with specialist or technical matters, so it is easy to fall into the trap of using jargon. People do not always agree about what jargon actually is, but the following definition should help:

> Jargon is the use of specialist, technical, or 'in-group' words when ordinary words would do the same job. It tends to make a text less effective because it alienates a significant number of readers who find it irritating or pretentious.

Sometimes, of course, you will have to use technical terms. If you are talking about the pollution of water supplies then you may have to refer to 'bromate concentrations', 'monitoring', and 'carcinogens'. If there is a likelihood that your report will be read by people who are unfamiliar with these terms, however, you should either explain them as you go along or make sure that there is an explanatory glossary in an appendix at the end of the report.

The same applies to acronyms. You and your colleagues may be very familiar with a range of acronyms that you use every day. They are short and convenient. Not everyone who reads your report will be as familiar with them, and you should allow for this when you write. It is advisable to take a belt-and-braces approach to this:

- The first time you use the name of an organization or anything that has been 'acronymized', write it out in full, followed by the acronym in brackets:
  It is a question of how the Drinking Water Inspectorate (DWI) and the Department of the Environment, Transport and the Regions (DETR) will react.

- In an appendix, make a list of all acronyms used with a translation.

To sum up ...

1 Writing is a process of gradually refining your words until they express accurately exactly what you wish to say. This process is called drafting.

2 You need to work on your text at different levels.

3 Begin by writing a first draft.

4 Then make any changes necessary to the structure.

5 Next consider your paragraphing. Paragraphs are the link between the overall structure and the content of individual sentences.

6 You may find you have to rework some of your sentences to ensure that they express your thought accurately.

7 Finally, examine your vocabulary and check that you have chosen words that are the most suitable for your subject matter and your readership.

7 Editing the report

CONTENTS

Editing is not the same as drafting **72**

Why editing is essential **73**

Structure **73**

Detailed cutting and rewriting **77**

Who does what and when **80**

To sum up … **81**

Editing is not the same as drafting

Editing involves looking at the report and thinking about how it can be improved. Drafting, too, involves reading what you have written and thinking about how it can be improved. So what's the difference? It is a question of focus. When you draft you are thinking about yourself as writer: about what you want to communicate to your audience. When you edit, you think about your readers: you try to see things from their point of view.

It is important to understand this distinction, because unless you do, you will find it hard to edit what you have written. In many ways the person who wrote a text is the worst person to be given the job of editing it. They have been working at it for hours, days—months, even—and find it difficult to stand back from it and look at it objectively and dispassionately. That is exactly what an editor has to do, but it is something that the author finds very difficult to achieve. (That's why, when I have finished writing this book, I shall hand it over—with some relief—to a professional editor, who will look at it with fresh eyes.)

How you tackle the issue of editing will depend on your working circumstances. If you are a member of a work group or committee, you will have a different approach from if you are working on your own. We'll look at these issues later in the chapter. For now, let's consider why and how we edit.

Why editing is essential

Editing is the process by which the author's final draft is made ready to be published in a form that the reader can read and understand as easily as possible. It forms part of this workflow:

Planning

Drafting

Editing

Publishing

Reading

See Chapter 8, Presentation

By publishing I mean the process of presenting the report on paper or in an electronic form, so that it can be accessed by readers. This process forms the subject matter of the next chapter.

So there are two parts to the editing process:

- improving the text so that it is as accessible as possible;

- preparing the text for print or electronic delivery.

This chapter concentrates on the first of these two. The second is covered in Chapter 8. Like drafting, editing is concerned with structure and expression. It is also concerned with technical accuracy.

Structure

The original structure of the report was produced as part of the planning stage. We looked at typical structures in Chapter 5. It may then have been modified during the drafting stage, if you found that it was—for whatever reason—unsatisfactory. Throughout this period the changes you made will probably have been determined by the report's content—what it is you wanted to say. Now you need to look at it from a different perspective. The content is by now very familiar to you. But much of it will be new to the reader. Does the structure of the report allow for this? Does it make it as easy as possible for the reader to grasp all this new material?

Ordering

A report should present information to the reader in the order that is easiest for the reader. Too often one reads reports that reflect how the writer writes rather than how the reader reads. Although you have collected the information in a particular order, that is not necessarily the best order in which to present it to the reader. For example, the pressure group report described in Chapter 2 chooses a simple historical/geographical structure. It shows how the present situation arose, and follows the unfortunate women caught up in the sex trade from Moldova through to Italy. This is almost certainly very different from the order in which the writer(s) accumulated this information, but it is a very good structure for the reader. Your aim should be to achieve a structure that readers will find equally easy to follow.

See pages 15–16.

This means that, if possible, items that are similar should be arranged together and sequenced so that one flows neatly on to the next. If a lot of information is being presented, it should build as a set of logically linked items, rather than as a heap that has just been thrown together.

Like this:

rather than like this:

You should also consider whether there are any obstructions to the smooth flow of ideas and information. Sometimes writers are so keen to include every small detail of information they have accumulated that the report becomes difficult or impossible to read. This is illustrated in the example opposite.

A breakdown by country of residence of inbound tourists shows that, in 1992, the United Kingdom ranked first with 28%, followed by Germany with 19%. However, current trends indicate that the share of British visitors has declined slightly, while that of German visitors has grown.

Other important countries of residence of tourists are Spain (11% in 1992), the Netherlands (10%), and France (7%). Unlike other tourists, Spaniards opt for short visits rather than package holidays. Demand by visitors from certain Scandinavian countries is significant. Finland (4%) and Sweden (3%) accounted for 7% of the nights spent by non-residents. The most important non-European country of residence is the United States, which accounted for 2% of the non-resident demand in 1992.

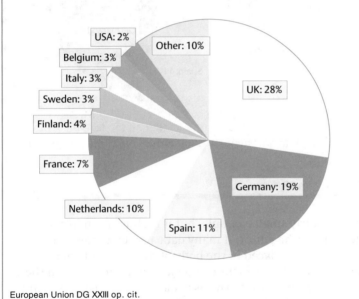

European Union DG XXIII op. cit.

The text adds almost nothing to our understanding of the chart. If you have numerical data it is a good idea to express it visually, as is done here. But once that has been done the purpose of the accompanying text is to draw the reader's attention to what is significant about the data. You could say, for example:

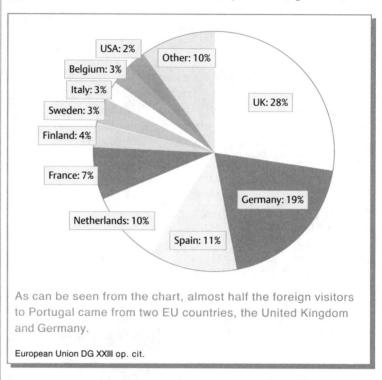

As can be seen from the chart, almost half the foreign visitors to Portugal came from two EU countries, the United Kingdom and Germany.

European Union DG XXIII op. cit.

This is a fairly small example, but it highlights an important question for the editor: If many data are being presented, should they be placed in the body of the report or should they be placed in a separate appendix and referred to in the narrative of the report? This is a question of judgement, and you will be helped considerably if you put yourself in the place of the reader.

There is a further question for the editor to consider: Is all this detail really necessary?

Detailed cutting and rewriting

Most writers write too much rather than too little, and it is an important part of the editor's job to cut unnecessary material, whether it is data or words. Reports should be as short as is compatible with providing readers with a clear argument or narrative and the essential detailed information to support it.

As you edit the report you may find that there are whole sections which can be removed without harming the report. They will often signal themselves as an interruption or hiccup in the flow of the narrative. Try reading the report without them and judge how much is lost. If you are uncertain, consider the halfway house of putting such material in an appendix and simply refer-ring to it at the point from which you removed it. (And, at a later stage in the editing, ask yourself: If I put this material in an appendix, will anyone read it? If not, does it matter?)

More often, the question is more complex than simply: Should I cut out this section? You find that a section contains a mass of material, some of which is relevant and some of which is not. Then you have to combine cutting some material and rewriting the whole in order to simplify and clarify the message that is conveyed.

The next two pages are based on a fuller version of the text quoted on page 75. It is the section on Portugal from an EU statistical report on tourism in the period 1980–92. On page 78 is most of the original text with the accompanying charts removed and a short section of text cut for reasons of space. The problem with this text is that it contains so much detail that it is difficult to read and interpret. On page 79 it has been rewritten and two of the original charts reinstated to accompany and enhance the text rather than just providing a parallel set of information as they did in the original.

A breakdown by country of residence of inbound tourists shows that, in 1992, the United Kingdom ranked first with 28%, followed by Germany with 19%. However, current trends indicate that the share of British visitors has declined slightly, while that of German visitors has grown. Other important countries of residence of tourists are Spain (11% in 1992), the Netherlands (10%), and France (7%). Unlike other tourists, Spaniards opt for short visits rather than package holidays. Demand by visitors from certain Scandinavian countries is significant. Finland (4%) and Sweden (3%) accounted for 7% of the nights spent by non-residents. The most important non-European country of residence is the United States, which accounted for 2% of the non-resident demand in 1992.

Throughout the 1980s the annual net occupancy rate for hotels and similar establishments showed little variation. The downturn in the late 1980s and early 1990s reflects the general slowdown in mass tourism to the Mediterranean countries and the increase in accommodation supply. The total number of nights spent in officially registered accommodation establishments increased from 24.8 million in 1980 to 36.9 million in 1992. But it was not a steady rise, because the rates dipped between 1986 and 1989 due to a slowdown in mass tourism throughout Europe in the late 1980s and rebounded in 1990–1991. The figures do not include data on non-registered establishments, for which there is high demand in Portugal. The total number of nights would almost double to an estimated 67 million if non-registered establishments were also considered.

In 1980 residents outnumbered non-residents for nights spent at tourist accommodations. Non-residents subsequently narrowed the gap: in 1982 they exceeded 50% and by 1991 their share reached 62%, falling back to 59.5% in 1992.

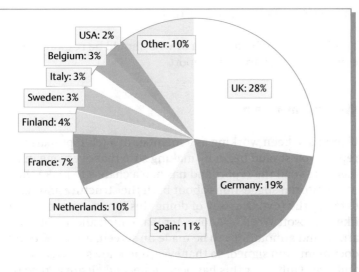

As can be seen from the chart above, almost half the foreign visitors to Portugal came from two EU countries, the United Kingdom and Germany.

Throughout the 1980s hotels were able to maintain the proportion of their rooms they were able to fill. The proportion went down in the late 1980s and early 1990s because more hotels were built, while Mediterranean tourism declined.

Between 1980 and 1992 the total number of nights spent in hotels increased by almost 50%, with a slowdown between 1986 and 1989. The chart below shows that between 1985 and 1992 non-residents spent more time in all types of accommodation than residents, and the gap between the two groups tended to widen.

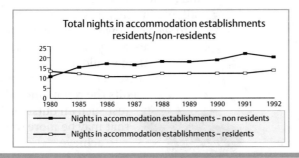

| # Who does what and when

This leads on to the question of who should be responsible for editing the final draft of a report.

Working in a team

If you have been working as a member of a team preparing the report, you should begin by making sure that everyone in the team has read the report and has had a chance to make their own editorial suggestions about both the structure and the detail of the text. One way of doing this is to use a programme like Microsoft Word or Adobe Acrobat which allows for alterations and annotations to be made on screen, attached to the document, and signed, so that everyone knows who says what and why. Only after this has been done, and all are agreed on the final text, should you move to the next stage.

A second pair of eyes

If at all possible you should make sure that the report is read by someone who has had nothing to do with its preparation, but has some background knowledge of the subject. This reader should come to it with none of the attitudes and preconceptions of the writers. He or she will know nothing of the problems you have faced and the difficulties you have overcome. So you will get a response that reflects the interests and concerns of the reader rather than those of the writer. Ask your reader to be completely honest about their response and to give you comments that are as detailed as time allows. In this way you will be helped to see your own project with fresh eyes, and much more objectively than would otherwise be the case. Ideally the person who edits the report should be just such an outsider, but that may be more difficult to achieve.

Working alone

If you are unable to find anyone at all from 'outside' to read the report (for reasons of confidentiality, for example), then you should try to allow enough time to do the following. Put the report on one side for as long as you can. Then get on with something completely different (or as different as possible) and try to forget all about it. The longer you can leave before returning to the text the better. You should find when you re-read it that you notice all sorts of things that you had missed before. Some sections which you thought were fine will now seem muddled and cluttered; other sections you had struggled with and found less satisfactory will now appear clearer than you had remembered. In this frame of mind you can set about the task of editing.

To sum up ...

1 If you are working as a member of a team, make sure that all members of the team are happy with the final draft *before* you proceed to have it edited.

2 It is very important to have the final draft read (and if possible edited) by someone who has not been involved in its production.

3 If you have to edit your own work, try to leave as long as possible between completing the final draft and starting to edit it. This will help you to be more objective.

4 Drafting is the process by which you work from a first text to the final draft. Editing is what you do to the final draft to make it ready for the reader.

5 You should begin by working on the structure. Make sure that it is clear, flows well, and is comprehensible to the reader.

6 Then work on the text paragraph by paragraph. Look to cut and rewrite whenever you think that the text is too dense with detail, especially where statistics are concerned.

8 Presentation

CONTENTS

The importance of
presentation **82**

Typeface **84**

Headings **87**

Space **88**

To sum up ... **88**

The importance of presentation

When you have planned, written, and edited your report, it is tempting to think that your work is done.

It isn't.

Like any other form of writing, writing a report is a form of communication. If you take little care over the presentation of your report, then it will fail to have the impact it deserves. To see how this works, compare these two versions of the same extract from a report.

The second is not just more attractive to look at, but is also much easier to read. This is because attention has been paid to:

■ **typeface**
The first example is printed in a traditional typewriter style font called Courier. It is not particularly easy to read or attractive. The second is in a much more attractive and read-able typeface, Garamond.

■ **headings**
There are headings in the first example, but because they are printed in exactly the same way as the rest of the text, they don't stand out and so fail in their purpose. In the second text the headings are clear and eye-catching.

■ **space**
The first example is cramped and uninviting. The second makes good use of white space and attracts the eye.

```
Working Party on Remuneration and Appraisal
Report
Executive Summary
1. Remuneration
At present the remuneration of all staff (except
the Chief Executive) is set by the Executive and is
ultimately the responsibility of the Chief
Executive. His remuneration is set by the Board. If
these two processes get out of phase there is a
danger that either the differential between the
remuneration of the Chief Executive and his senior
managers is seriously eroded, or the Chief
Executive's freedom of action is severely limited.
The Working Party came to the conclusion that there
needed to be some formal arrangement to oversee
all remuneration within the company and thus avoid
that danger.
```

Working Party on Remuneration and Appraisal

Report

Executive Summary

1 Remuneration

At present the remuneration of all staff (except the Chief Executive) is set by the Executive and is ultimately the responsibility of the Chief Executive. His remuneration is set by the Board. If these two processes get out of phase there is a danger that either the differential between the remuneration of the Chief Executive and his senior managers is seriously eroded, or the Chief Executive's freedom of action is severely limited. The Working Party came to the conclusion that there needed to be some formal arrangement to oversee all remuneration within the company and thus avoid that danger.

Typeface

With modern computers and software, you have available to you a considerable array of different typefaces, or fonts as they are often called. It is tempting to experiment and produce text that is exotic, bizarre, or just plain ugly. So it helps to have a clear idea of what fonts can—and cannot—do.

Fonts can be divided into three broad categories: display, script, and text. As the name suggests, display fonts are used when you want to draw attention to the type itself—in adverts and posters for example. In text they have a limited use, but some can be used for eye-catching headings. These are some examples:

ABCDEF   ABCDEF   **Abcdef**

As you can see from this example, fonts of this type are not well suited to the presentation of texts of any length. They are difficult to read and the effort soon becomes irritating.

There is little place for such typefaces in the presentation of reports.

Script fonts simulate a range of different types of handwriting:

Abcdef   Abcdef   *Abcdef*

Script fonts have an informal look which may be useful in personal letters, but they are not much use in a report.

It is text fonts with which we are mainly concerned. They can be divided into two broad groups:

serif—like this

sans serif—like this

The serifs are the little bits that stick out at the top and bottom of the uprights of the letters, and at the ends of the strokes making up letters like 's'. Traditionally, serif fonts are used in the printing of extended texts because they are considered to be easier to read. Sans serif fonts are considered to be less formal. They are very useful for captions and headings.

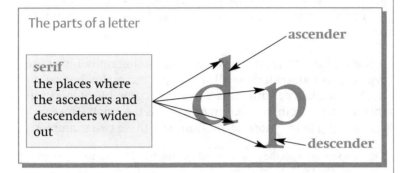

The parts of a letter

ascender

serif
the places where
the ascenders and
descenders widen
out

descender

Size

When you tell your computer to present text in a particular font, you also need to specify the size you want and the spacing between lines of text. The size of a font is measured in units called points. This is the measurement from the top of an ascender to the bottom of a descender. The gap between the lines (called the 'leading', pronounced 'ledding') is also measured in points. You measure from the bottom of one descender to the top of an ascender in the line below. This gives you a measurement that includes the size of the font and the size of the gap between the lines. Type and leading are usually described by giving the type size, followed by a figure produced by adding the leading to the type size. So the example below shows OUP Swift 36/43 ('36 on 43'):

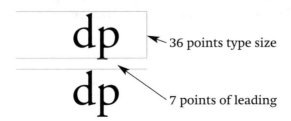

36 points type size

7 points of leading

| # Readability

The aim above all is to make sure that your text is readable. This is not a judgement on its style or grammar; it is a measure of how easy readers find it to decode the text when reading at speed. Choosing the right font helps considerably. Some fonts are much easier to read than others, which is why they crop up over and over again in printed material. But size is important as well.

It is important to get the type size and leading right. If you use type that is too small you will save paper but make the text difficult to read. In certain fonts 9 point is acceptable (it works in this book, for example), but in others it is too small. The correct leading helps enormously. Compare these two examples:

> It is important to get the type size and leading right. If you use type that is too small you will save paper but make the text difficult to read. In certain fonts 9 point is acceptable (it works in this book, for example), but in others it is too small. The correct leading helps enormously.

> It is important to get the type size and leading right. If you use type that is too small you will save paper but make the text difficult to read. In certain fonts 9 point is acceptable (it works in this book, for example), but in others it is too small. The correct leading helps enormously.

Both examples are in 9 point Times, but the first is 9/9, while the second is 9/12. As you can see, the first is much harder to read than the second. If you don't specify a font size and leading the computer will use its default sizes. These will usually work quite well, but it is useful to understand how to change them to achieve the effect you want.

The other feature you need consider is line length. Lines that are too short or too long are difficult to read. A good guide is that the average full line should contain between ten and fourteen words.

Headings

Headings help to break the text up and enable readers to find their way around the report more easily. A heading is distinguished from the text around it by:

- style (e.g. *italic* or <u>underline</u>);

- weight (e.g. **bold**);

- size;

- colour.

In a document of any length you will probably find that you need headings of different levels of importance. It is quite common to make use of three different levels of heading. In this book, for example, there are:

Chapter headings

A headings   ### B headings

The use of different levels means that you can indicate to the reader which parts of the report belong together and when you are starting on a major new section. For example, if you look back at this chapter you will see that it follows this structure:

In a well-organized report, the levels of heading should reflect the original outline. (See pages 53–4 for more about outlining.)

	Presentation		Level 1
The importance of presentation	Typeface	Headings	Level 2
	Size	Readability	Level 3

Reviewing your report and checking the levels of headings in this way is a useful method of ensuring that its structure is clear.

Space

Allied to the style, weight, and size of headings is the question of space. As you can see from the headings in this book, you can emphasize headings quite dramatically by the careful use of space before and after them. In general, the more important the heading the more space you should put around it. Generally you put more before it than you do after it.

Space is important throughout a report. The more you try to cram onto each page, the less attractive and the less readable the pages will become. The converse is true ... up to a point. You should have enough white space around your text to relax the eye and to make things easy to find. If you go beyond that point and let the white space dominate the page, readers will soon begin to find it irritating (and extravagant!). It's a question of judgement and moderation.

To sum up ...

1 If you want your report to be read and understood by readers and wish to avoid their frustration, think carefully about how it is presented.

2 You should choose a clear typeface, normally with serifs, and a suitable size, between 9 and 12 points.

3 The leading (gap between the lines of type) should be big enough to aid readability.

4 Careful use of headings is also important. You will normally find that you need three or four levels of heading, distinguished by one or more of font, size, weight, colour.

5 Make sure that headings are allowed enough space. This applies to the document as a whole: avoid squashing too much onto each page.

These points (and some others) are illustrated in the diagram opposite.

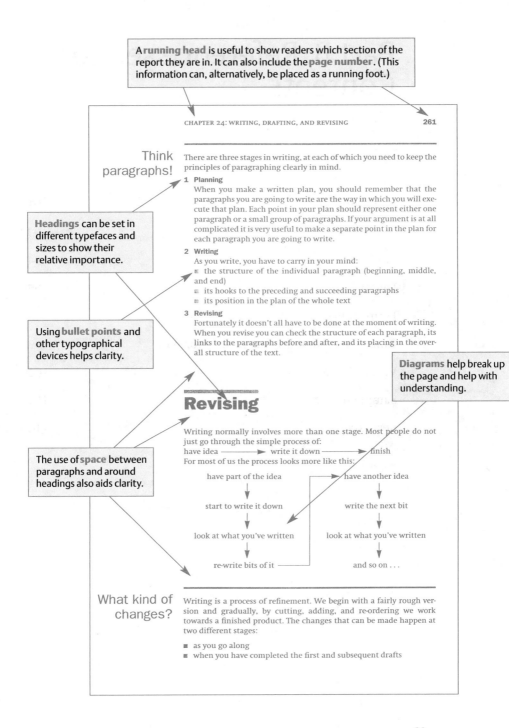

A **running head** is useful to show readers which section of the report they are in. It can also include the **page number**. (This information can, alternatively, be placed as a running foot.)

Think paragraphs!

Headings can be set in different typefaces and sizes to show their relative importance.

Using **bullet points** and other typographical devices helps clarity.

The use of **space** between paragraphs and around headings also aids clarity.

Diagrams help break up the page and help with understanding.

There are three stages in writing, at each of which you need to keep the principles of paragraphing clearly in mind.

1 Planning
When you make a written plan, you should remember that the paragraphs you are going to write are the way in which you will execute that plan. Each point in your plan should represent either one paragraph or a small group of paragraphs. If your argument is at all complicated it is very useful to make a separate point in the plan for each paragraph you are going to write.

2 Writing
As you write, you have to carry in your mind:
- the structure of the individual paragraph (beginning, middle, and end)
- its hooks to the preceding and succeeding paragraphs
- its position in the plan of the whole text

3 Revising
Fortunately it doesn't all have to be done at the moment of writing. When you revise you can check the structure of each paragraph, its links to the paragraphs before and after, and its placing in the overall structure of the text.

Revising

Writing normally involves more than one stage. Most people do not just go through the simple process of:

have idea ⟶ write it down ⟶ finish

For most of us the process looks more like this:

have part of the idea ⟶ have another idea

start to write it down → write the next bit

look at what you've written → look at what you've written

re-write bits of it → and so on . . .

What kind of changes?

Writing is a process of refinement. We begin with a fairly rough version and gradually, by cutting, adding, and re-ordering we work towards a finished product. The changes that can be made happen at two different stages:

- as you go along
- when you have completed the first and subsequent drafts

Part B: Reference section
Contents

The commission   91

Audience   93

Purpose   94

Length   95

Permanence   98

Language guidelines: formal or informal?   99

Visual presentation   102

Sample reports   109

Resources   116

The commission

Use the checklist below to make sure that you have thought through all aspects of the commission. Use a copy of the form on the next page to list the key features.

Checklist

Tick when you have answered these questions:

Audience

☐ At whom is your report aimed?

☐ Who else may read it?

☐ How formal or informal should it be?

Purpose

☐ What is its main purpose?

☐ What are its secondary purposes?

Remit

☐ Have you got a written remit? If not, can you express the remit in two or three clear sentences?

☐ How long have you got to complete the report?

☐ Are you working alone? If not, who are you working with?

☐ Whom are you required to consult?

☐ What will the status of the report be?

☐ How long should it be?

Audience

Main audience:

Other possible readers:

Tone: Informal / Semi-informal / Semi-formal / Formal

(Delete as appropriate)

Purpose

Main purpose:

Subsidiary purpose(s):

Remit

Attach, or write here:

Time available:

Work group:

People to consult:

Status:

Length:

Audience

Use this chart to guide you towards defining who you are writing for. But remember that it's only a guide and that these aren't hard-and-fast categories.

Audience contains	Approach
Close colleagues, people you work with regularly. People with whom you share thoughts, ideas, language. People whose reaction to things you can normally predict. (People who understand—and appreciate—your jokes!)	**Informal**: You can assume that your audience shares quite a lot of your knowledge and attitudes. You can adopt a relaxed and friendly manner in your writing. You can address them as 'you' and talk about yourself as 'I'. You can use contractions ('can't', 'we'd', etc.).
People in your company or organization, whose work/activities you are familiar with but whom you don't know well personally. People whom you would normally speak to in a relaxed and not very formal way.	**Semi-informal**: Your audience knows and understands the organization, so don't be 'stuffed shirt' with them. Use language that is relaxed but not familiar. Move away from using 'you' and 'I'.
People inside or outside your organization whose work/activities you know about but are not familiar with. If you were speaking to them as a group you'd try to get them to unbend and relax, but not too much. You have no reason to believe that they'd be hostile to what you have to say.	**Semi-formal**: You don't know these people, so don't try to pretend that you do. On the other hand they aren't complete strangers, so don't treat them with heavy formality. Keep your language friendly but neutral.
People you don't really know at all. The general public. People who might be friendly or hostile to what you have to say—you have no way of knowing.	**Formal**: This is language on its best behaviour. You don't know what will happen to your report after it leaves your hands, so avoid any kind of language that may offend those who are looking for things to criticize!

Purpose

You need a clear definition of the purpose of your document. This diagram shows the three main purposes of reports. Your document may contain a mix of different proportions of each.

To inform
You know something your readers don't. Your purpose is to give them that information as clearly and concisely as possible. This involves not just factual statements but also interpretation to help them grasp the relative significance of different pieces of information.

To record
The information in your report will be needed at some point(s) in the future. It provides a picture of how things are at this point in time. It may be read by people who don't have the background information you possess.

To persuade
The purpose of your report is to lead to action of some kind. You have to provide an interpretation of the available information which makes it possible for a decision to be made. The report may offer a choice (with the pros and cons for each option) or strongly urge one course of action.

Length

It is highly desirable to decide in advance how long your report should be. The categories in this chart are designed to give some idea of the options, and to emphasize the point that the longer the report, the more sophisticated the structure needs to be.

Type	Structure
Short up to 2,000 words, or 3 pages	No need for an elaborate structure. Begin with a heading to define the subject, possibly followed by a sentence to define it in more detail. Introduce the approach adopted in the report in a single paragraph. Then develop the subject in a series of linked paragraphs. Conclude with one or two paragraphs summing up the main points. (Or list these as a series of bullet points.)
Medium 2,000–10,000 words, or 4–20 pages	Even at the lower end, this size of report is making demands on the reader's time. So devote the first page to a brief summary, preferably using bullet points. Recommendations for action can also be listed on this page, if appropriate. The body of the report then begins on page 2. If the report contains any detailed information (especially numerical), put this in one or more appendices and refer to these in the body of the report.
Long Over 10,000 words, or over 20 pages	This length requires a more elaborate structure. It definitely needs a summary at the beginning, but with long reports this may be more than one page—it may be an introductory chapter. It will also almost certainly have appendices for detailed and statistical information. In addition consider: • a table of contents at the beginning; • a preface which outlines the remit of the report and names of those involved in preparing it; • an index at the end; • a list of resources used; • the use of a numbering system (1.1, 1.2, 1.2.1, 1.2.2, etc.).

| # Template for medium-length report

First page

- title;

- date;

- bulleted/numbered list of main findings;

- bulleted/numbered list of recommendations.

Body of the report

- introduction
  - remit
  - person(s) responsible for report
  - brief list of main sources of information (if detailed, put in full in appendix);

- main section 1
  - introductory paragraph outlining content of section
  - series of paragraphs containing:
    - information
    - interpretation
    - recommendations (if any);

- other main sections as necessary;

- conclusion—account of main findings of report in continuous prose.

Appendices

A report of this length probably won't have many. Possible candidates:

- detailed numerical data and/or charts and tables;

- list of people, institutions and publications consulted.

General

Some form of numbering is essential. Certainly pages should be numbered, and probably sections and sub-sections should be allocated numbers too.

Template for long report

Reports over twenty pages or 10,000 words will have some or all of the following:

Preliminaries

- title page giving title, author(s), and name of the organization responsible;
- contents page;
- page detailing remit;
- short chapter listing main findings and recommendations.

Body of the report

Series of chapters, each of which contains:

- introduction outlining the content of this part of the information;
- body of the chapter containing evidence and interpretation of it;
- conclusion highlighting most important findings and recommendations.

Appendices

- numerical data;
- maps, diagrams, and illustrations that don't *have* to be in the body of the report;
- extended quotations from documents;
- detailed list of people and organizations consulted;
- detailed list of printed and other documents consulted;
- lists of acronyms used.

Index

Permanence

Think about how permanent you want the contents of your report to be. Of course you can never tell: once you have distributed it, you have no control over what people do with it. But some idea of its relative permanence will give you an idea of how much background information and other details you need to include.

Temporary
Your report is intended to be read, acted upon, and then discarded. (But remember that, in most organizations, if decisions of any importance are being made, a copy will be filed in order to establish a 'paper trail' in case of later problems. If this is at all likely, then regard your report as semi-permanent.) You can assume that your readers understand much of the background to the report. You only need to include details that are directly relevant to it.

Semi-permanent
Your report will be fairly widely distributed and will be filed. But its purpose is mainly to inform and make recommendations. So it will eventually become outdated and obsolete (or superseded by a new report on the same subject). But its greater lifespan means that not everyone who reads it will know all the background. This may entail a certain amount of explanation. You also need to make sure that all relevant details are included, probably in the form of appendices.

Permanent
Any report that has, as one of its aims, to record a set of information for future use falls into this category. Those reading it in later years will be researching information, but may not be aware of the whole background to your report. So you need to give a full and detailed background, and to refer the reader to other related reports (e.g. your report may be one of a series). In future years your report may be the only source of detailed information for people researching in this area, so you should think carefully about the details to include and how to present them—even detailed appendices may need some explanatory background information. It's also very important to give a clear account of the methodology by which the report was produced—and the names of those responsible and those consulted.

Language guidelines: formal or informal?

Words

When you are writing, you nearly always have a choice of words. How you exercise that choice has an important effect on how your report is received. If you are writing a formal or semi-formal report you should use appropriate vocabulary. For example:

Formal	Informal
experiment	take a crack give it a go
research	find out about
innovate	try something new

In dictionaries and other word reference books, informal words and expressions are often marked:

inf. (informal)
colloq. (colloquial—which means much the same)
sl. (slang)
taboo (this refers to words that cause offence in certain social groups)

Jargon

The *Concise Oxford Dictionary* defines this as:

> words or expressions used by a particular profession or group that are difficult for others to understand.

and notes that originally it meant 'twittering, chattering', later 'gibberish'. **AVOID!**

Pronouns

Pronouns are words that stand in for nouns and other words and groups of words to help us avoid repetition. The commonest are the personal pronouns:

I   we   you   he   she   it   they

and related forms ('me', 'us') and pronouns ('mine', 'ours', etc.). In formal reports you should avoid using 'I', 'we', and 'you', because using them gives the writing a direct and personal tone which is quite informal. In informal reports, on the other hand, using them is normal, and not to do so can sometimes seem over-formal.

If you are accustomed to writing in a direct and personal way, you may need to do a little 'translating', when revising your first draft:

Personal	Impersonal
I am certain	it is clear
we consider that	the committee considers that

and so on.

'He', 'she', or 'it'

While considering pronouns you also need to be aware of the 'he'/'she' trap. Using 'he' all through a document to refer to both men and women is far less common these days than it used to be, but it still happens and still gives offence. Writing 'he or she' every time is wearisome and irritating for the reader. These are some other solutions:

- Turn the sentence into the plural (instead of writing, 'Every officer should check his/her ...', write, 'All officers should check their ...')

- Use 'they', 'them', 'their' even with singular sentences. ('Every officer should check their ...') **But** some traditionalists object to this, so if you are writing for a particularly stuffy audience, be careful.

Grammar and formality

As you've probably observed, this book is written in a fairly informal style, as are others in this series. This is the result of a deliberate choice, and it is interesting to observe how it is done.

On the whole the authors of these books haven't used particularly informal vocabulary, but we have made use of the personal pronouns 'I', 'we', and 'you', in order to give the impression of speaking directly to you, the reader. Another thing we have done is to make use of contractions.

Contractions

When we speak, we run words together. So, instead of saying 'is not' we often say 'isn't'. English has a well-known way of writing down these contracted forms, using an apostrophe to represent the missing letter(s). Using contractions in written English brings it closer to speech, and makes it less formal. So, if you are writing a formal report, don't use contractions.

Other speech elements

In general, the more your written sentences are like the patterns of spoken English the less formal they are. In speech we make use of 'sentences' that are incomplete, for example 'sentences' without verbs. Like this. In informal writing this is acceptable (although if you do it too much it becomes irritating for the reader). But you should avoid such 'sentences' in a formal report. Similarly, you may have noticed that in this book I sometimes begin sentences with words like 'but' and 'and'. This, too, is a mark of informal writing. Traditionally you should only use 'and' and 'but' to join other words or groups of words within a sentence. Again, if you are writing formally, don't begin sentences with 'and', 'but', 'or'.

Visual presentation

Reports present complex and detailed information and their interpretation. An important feature of this communication process is the use of visuals. We can use illustrations, charts, and diagrams to present a wide range of information.

Figures

Business people are accustomed to the use of charts and diagrams to present numerical information in a way that makes it easier to understand and assimilate. These methods are not always so familiar to those outside the world of business and finance. The simpler types of numerical chart are, however, very useful in a wide range of applications.

Suppose, for example, a school has the following data about one year's examination entries and the grades achieved:

Subject	Total	A	B	C	D	E	F
English	173	15	27	42	35	33	21
Maths	164	10	23	56	43	29	3
Science	153	22	34	31	33	21	12
French	108	11	24	46	13	9	5
Geography	116	3	9	47	39	14	4
History	119	1	7	29	22	45	15
Total	833	62	124	251	185	151	60

There are various ways in which the head teacher could present this information to the public.

Column chart

As the name suggests, this presents data as a series of columns. The higher the column, the bigger the number. So the English exam grades could be presented like this:

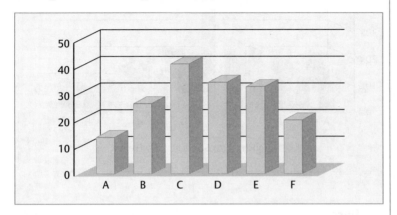

We can also use a column chart to compare sets of data. The table below shows the actual numbers of passes at each level in three subjects:

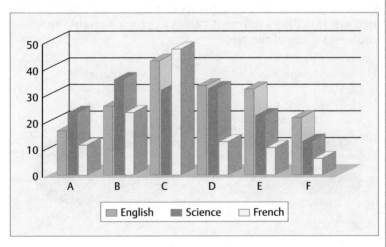

A comparison of raw data like this is not as helpful, however, as one in which we express the numbers for each grade as a percentage of the total entry. This is shown in the chart at the top of the next page.

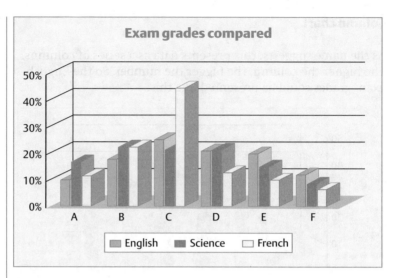

Pie chart

What is interesting about this kind of comparison is how likely a student is to get a good grade in a particular subject. Another way of presenting this kind of data is in a pie chart. As its name suggests, this shows different values as proportions of the whole—as slices of the pie:

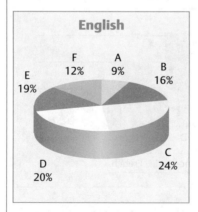

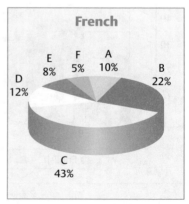

You only have to compare the A, B, and C segments of the two diagrams to see how much more successful French has been than English.

Line chart

A line chart is useful if you want to show how things have progressed over a period of time:

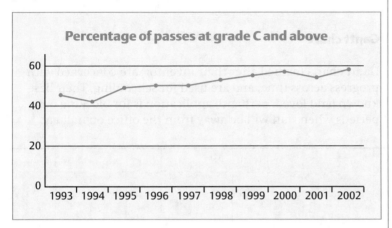

You can also use a column chart for the same purpose. Here we present on the same chart the percentage of passes at A–C and the total number of candidates entered:

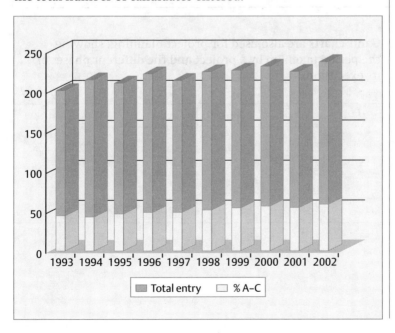

| # Other data

We can present information that is not numerical (or a combination of numerical and non-numerical information) visually.

Gantt chart

Gantt charts (named after their inventor) are concerned with progress across time, and are used for scheduling. Their best-known (and loved, perhaps!) application is for blocking out periods when staff will be away from the office on holiday:

	Jan	Feb	Mar	Apr	May	June	July	Aug	Sept	Oct	Nov	Dec
George			▓▓▓								▌	
Elwyn					▓▓			▓▓				
Maria				▌		▓▓						
Debbie				▌		▓▓▓						
Shaun							▌			▓▓▓		

Gantt charts are also used for project planning, showing the period taken up by a project and the different phases of its execution:

	Jan	Feb	Mar	Apr	May	June
Research	▓▓▓					
Detailed planning		▓▓▓				
Recruitment			▓▓▓			
Training				▓▓▓▓▓		

Flowchart

If you want to show a process diagrammatically, you can use a flowchart. This term is used to cover a range of different diagrams. The one we are concerned with here is defined by the *Concise Oxford Dictionary* as:

> a diagram of a sequence of movements or actions making up a complex system.

So if we wanted to show in a diagram the sequence of actions required to cook spiced lentils, we might begin like this:

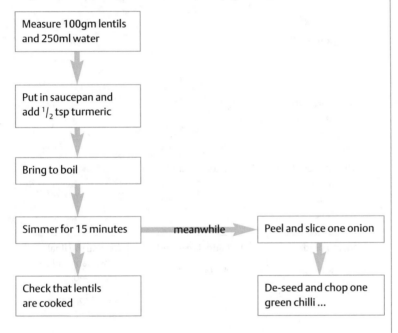

The diagram reads from top to bottom and the split indicates a second set of actions to be completed while one of the first set is in progress.

Decision chart

A decision chart is a diagram that helps the reader go through a series of choices in order to come to a decision. It can, for example, be used to give a graphic demonstration of a set of rules. The example below explains how to spell verbs when you add the letters '-ing' or '-ed'.

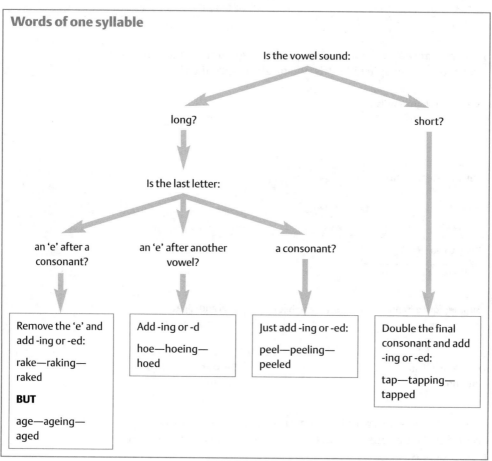

Words of one syllable

Is the vowel sound:

long? short?

Is the last letter:

an 'e' after a consonant? | an 'e' after another vowel? | a consonant?

Remove the 'e' and add -ing or -ed:

rake—raking—raked

BUT

age—ageing—aged

Add -ing or -d

hoe—hoeing—hoed

Just add -ing or -ed:

peel—peeling—peeled

Double the final consonant and add -ing or -ed:

tap—tapping—tapped

Sample reports

Brief formal report

Nike (UK) Ltd

Complaint: Objection to a magazine advertisement that showed four winning golfers. Two were shown winning once, one twice, and Tiger Woods three times. All except one were wearing Nike branded clothing. Next to the pictures the captions stated: 'Did you know he hadn't won in six years? Did you know he won three straight? Did you know this was his first professional repeat? Did you know ... OK, you knew this one. Did you know he won back to back? Did you know ... OK, you knew this one too.' The advertisement claimed: 'The Nike Tour Accuracy. Did you know that the Nike Tour Accuracy is better off the tee, through the wind and around the greens?' The complainant objected that the advertisement misleadingly implied that Tiger Woods used the advertised balls, whereas he used a modified version.

Adjudication: Complaint not upheld

The advertisers said the Tour Accuracy golf ball that was for sale and the Tour Accuracy golf ball used by Tiger Woods used the same ball technology. They shared the same injection moulded construction, urethane materials, manufacturing process, ball size, core size, cover thickness, tooling dimple number and pattern, and mantle layers. They said the only differences in the ball used by Tiger Woods were a slightly harder cover and slightly softer core, which were needed to accommodate his 125 mph swing speed. The minor adjustments made for Tiger Woods' extraordinarily powerful swing speed were designed to compensate for his unique capabilities. The advertisers maintained that the similar properties of both balls meant in practice their performance was almost identical. They pointed out that the modifications made to the ball for Tiger Woods had been widely reported in the golf press and provided copies of some of those articles as verification of that fact. The advertisers asserted that it was standard practice for professional golfers to have individual modifications made to their equipment, and that that was widely reported in the press and known by golfers, the target audience of the advertisement. The Authority considered that the advertisement implied that all four golfers used the advertised golf ball. It nevertheless concluded that most golfers would understand that professional golfers used modified equipment and that, because the advertised ball and the ball used by Tiger Woods were essentially the same, the advertisement was not misleading. The Authority asked the advertisers to take care in future not to state or imply that the equipment used by depicted winning golfers was exactly the same as that available to the general public.

(Advertising Standards Authority monthly report 116, January 2001)

Business committee report

Working Party on Remuneration and Appraisal

Report

Executive Summary

1 Remuneration

At present the remuneration of all staff (except the Chief Executive) is set by the Executive and is ultimately the responsibility of the Chief Executive. His remuneration is set by the Board. If these two processes get out of phase there is a danger that either the differential between the remuneration of the Chief Executive and his senior managers is seriously eroded, or the Chief Executive's freedom of action is severely limited. The Working Party came to the conclusion that there needed to be some formal arrangement to oversee all remuneration within the company and thus avoid that danger.

2 Appraisal

The Working Party examined the Company's new appraisal system introduced this year. The Board is responsible for appraising the Chief Executive and setting targets. At present there is no link between these two processes. The Working Party believes that they should be linked, so that the Chief Executive's targets can be reflected in those of his staff.

Recommendations

1 The Board should establish a Remuneration and Appraisal Committee to advise Directors on appraisal and remuneration within the Company.

2 The Remuneration and Appraisal Committee should be responsible for the Chief Executive's appraisal and target-setting. This process should take place in January and February of each year. The Committee should then make recommendations to the Board about the CEO's remuneration for the coming financial year.

Membership

The Working Party consisted of: James Blease, Fiona Martin, and Hilary McPhee.

Remit

1   To investigate how senior staff salaries and targets are determined at present and how performance is assessed.

2   To relate this process to the way in which the Chief Executive's salary and targets are determined and how his performance is assessed.

3   To take evidence from outside bodies, including organizations of comparable size and status to HomeAid, such as the General Housing Aid Council (GHAC), of how they approach these tasks.

4   To make recommendations to the Board of how the processes by which the salaries, targets, and performance assessments of the Chief Executive and senior managers can be improved and harmonized.

Evidence

The Working Party was advised by the Company's Chief Executive, its Human Resources Manager, and an external adviser, James Pearson of the recruitment company Executive Solutions. It also had documents on pay and appraisal from the Industrial Society, the City Bureau, and GHAC.

Remuneration

At present the setting of salaries and bonuses is the responsibility of the Chief Executive (except for his own remuneration, which is the responsibility of the Board). This has advantages and disadvantages. The Chief Executive knows what the Company can afford and he knows how well his staff are performing, so he is well placed to reward them both reasonably and fairly. On the other hand, if employees feel that they are being unfairly treated, the buck stops with him. There is also a large anomaly: if we are to maintain a reasonable differential between the salary of the Chief Executive and those of his senior managers, their salaries need to be taken into account when determining his. Otherwise an imbalance can be set up. At the moment, however, this is not done.

The Working Party reviewed HomeAid salaries. Most of the figures we were using date from March 2001. At that point the salaries of senior managers seemed to be in line with those of comparable grades in comparable companies. Those of junior grades, however, did seem to be on the low side. We found the multiplicity of grades difficult to grasp and didn't fully understand why it was necessary to have so many. HomeAid has 30 staff and no fewer than 9 staff grades and salary scales. There are 8 staff in 4 different 'Manager' grades which run from £20,000 to £70,000. The remaining 22 staff are on 5 grades which run from £11,500 to £26,000, with very considerable overlaps. Although this is strictly speaking outside our remit, we recommend to the Executive that they take another look at this system to see whether it isn't possible to achieve something that is simpler and clearer.

In the recent past the Board has had no clear set of arrangements for advising on salary structure or for determining rationally the remuneration of the Chief Executive. The Working Party recommends that:-

The Board should establish a Remuneration and Appraisal Committee to advise Directors on appraisal and remuneration within the Company.

While the composition of such a Committee is for the Board to determine, the Working Party would suggest that it should have strong links with the Finance Sub-Committee.

Appraisal

The Company has recently introduced a formal system of appraisal. 2001 saw the first round of appraisals, and clearly the system is still in its early stages and will develop and improve with experience. Every member of staff is appraised by his or her manager, with senior managers being appraised by the Chief Executive. Each person appraised is given a self-appraisal form some time before their appraisal. They complete this as preparation. It gives them an opportunity to express their own feelings about their job and how they are fulfilling it. The appraisal, too, is based on a form. This begins by listing the objectives that were set at the previous year's appraisal and provides for an assessment of how successful the person was at achieving each of these. The next stage is the setting of new objectives for the year ahead. These are agreed and signed by the manager and the employee, being later countersigned by the Chief Executive. The last page of the form is completed by the Manager and assesses the employee's performance under the headings of Job Knowledge, Teamwork, Dependability, Communication, and Attendance & Punctuality. For each there is a 5-point scale. The form concludes with an overall marking on a similar 5-point scale.

The logic of such a system is that the Chief Executive sets targets for his senior managers, who then do the same for their immediate subordinates and so on down the line. The principles are that: objectives should be attainable; they should be measurable; and they should be within the control of the employee.

It is provided in the Chief Executive's contract that his performance should also be assessed. There is, however, no link between this appraisal and the system now established within the rest of the Company. This is clearly illogical, since until the Chief Executive has his annual targets set he cannot realistically set those of his senior managers. This is scheduled for March each year.

The Working Party recommends, therefore that:- **The Remuneration and Appraisal Committee should be responsible for the Chief Executive's appraisal and target-setting. This process should take place in January and February of each year. The Committee should then make recommendations to the Board about the CEO's remuneration for the coming financial year.**

Although it is strictly outside the Working Party's remit, it was observed that there was scope for improving the present appraisal system:

● More thought could be given to the ways in which job descriptions and the setting of targets are related, with a view to making the system more homogeneous.

● The self-appraisal and appraisal forms could be more closely linked.

● Overall a greater emphasis on measurability would be helpful.

(This report has been adapted from one presented to a not-for-profit company. Names and some other details have been changed.)

Resources

Other books in the One Step Ahead series

Words by John Seely
Contains useful advice about vocabulary selection, formal and informal language, and jargon.

Spelling by Robert Allen
Not just the rules (although it lists all the useful ones), but also how to get a grip on and improve your spelling.

Punctuation by Robert Allen
How to punctuate better.

Editing and Revising Text by Jo Billingham
Covers the whole process of editing your own and other people's writing.

Online

Using a search engine like Google or Yahoo will raise hundreds of pages on report writing. Many of them are dedicated to specific fields, such as psychology or astronomy. As is always the case, the majority are US-based, so if you want to focus on the styles and approaches of your own country you need to filter accordingly. Two useful UK introductions to report-writing are:

www.surrey.ac.uk/Skills/Pack/report.html
This is part of a skills package for undergraduates, but contains advice that is useful for a wider audience, as well as download-able checklists and exercises.

www.sharedlearning.org.uk/
This site is aimed at people working in development, and there
are a series of screens on report writing. Again, its application
is wider than the target audience.

Permissions

We are grateful to the Advertising Standards Authority for
permission to quote the report on pages 109–10.

117

Index

Note: page numbers in **bold** indicate chapters and definitions

accuracy 69-70
acronyms 25, 71
additions 63
alone, working 35, 81
ambiguity avoidance 67
analytical approach 47
and, sentences beginning with 101
appendices 20, 28, 71, 77, **96, 97**
   and structure and planning 50, 51
argument 28, 48
audience/reader 7, 8, 91-2, **93**
   and editing 80
   as expert 22, 24-5
   mixed readership 26
   as reader 23-4
   skills 24-5
   writer's relationship with 25

basic pattern 49
beginnings 46, 49, 50
body and detail of report **96-7**
   excessive detail 28, 51, 74-6, 77-9
   samples 15, 18-19
   simplicity versus 50-1
   structure and planning 47, 48, 49, 50, 52
body of paragraph 64, 65
bold 87

brief reports, *see* short reports
bullet points 89, 97
business committee report 10, 16-19, **111-15**
but, sentences beginning with 101

chapters 97
   headings 87
charts **103-8**
   pie 75-6, 79, **104**
checkable information 8
chronological organisation 46
clarity 65, 66
coherence 65, 66
colloquial words 99
colour 87
column chart **103-4**
commission/remit 32-3, **91-2**
computers
   drafting with 53-4
   editing 80
   fonts, *see* typeface
   information storage 44
   online information 36, 42, 117-18
   publishing 28
   see also presentation
conciseness 65, 66
conclusions 96
   paragraph 64, 65
   samples 16, 19
   structure and planning 46, 47, 48, 49
conjunction, beginning sentence with 101

consumer research report 10, 13-14
contractions 101
conventions 8
Courier (font) 82-3
cuts 63, 77-9

decision charts **108**
defining project **22-34**
   reasons, *see* purpose
   remit 32-3, **91-2**
   see also audience
description 47
detail, *see* body and detail
diagrams 51, 89
   see also charts
display fonts 84
drafting 56-60
   and editing not same 56, 72
   example of 57-60
   redrafting, *see* revision
   see also levels of writing

editing **72-81**
   cutting and rewriting 77-9
   and drafting not same 56, 72
   essential 73
   ordering 63, 74-6
   responsibility for 80-1
   structure 73-6
electronic tools, *see* computers
evidence 7
examples, *see* sample reports
excessive detail and information 28, 51, 74-6, 77-9

executive summary and
recommendations for
action 8, 17, 29–30, 50, 97
expert, reader as 22, 24–5
exposition 47

figures **102–5**
see also charts; diagrams
first draft 58, 62
flexibility in planning 54–5
flowchart **107**
fonts, *see* typeface
formality 25, 26, 69, **93**
in brief report 10, 11–12,
109–11
in remit 33
words 25, **99–100**
'free-standing' report 31

Gantt chart **106**
Garamond (font) 82–3
grammar 67, **101**, 108
graphs 27, 51
groups, *see* teamwork

he/she/it problem 100
headings 50, 82–3, 87, **89**
human informants 36, 38–40

impersonal pronouns 100
improving text, *see* editing
index 97
informality 25, 69, **93**
fonts 85
words 25, **99–100**
information, *see* excessive
detail
information:
checkable 8
obtaining, *see* research
online 36, 42, 117–18
as purpose of report 27, **94**
recording and storing 43–4
interpretation 28
interviews, research 38–40
introductions 13, 16, 96
italic 87

jargon 70–1, **99**

language, *see* formality;
grammar; informality;
words
layout samples 14
lead sentence in paragraph
64, 65
leading (line gaps) 85–6
length:
of lines 86
of reports 33, **95**
long 50, **95**, **97**
medium **95–6**
see also short reports
of sentences 24, 25, 66–7
of words 24, 108
levels of writing and workflow
61–71
first draft 62
see also drafting; revision
line charts 79, **105**
line gap (leading) 85–6
line length 86
long reports 50, **95**, **97**
long sentences 24, 25, 66, 67
long subject of sentence 68
long words 24

main section, *see* body and
detail
medium-length reports **95–6**
multi-part reports 50

narrative 46, 49
nouns and noun phrases 67
numbering pages and sections
89, 96

one syllable words 108
ordering 63, 74–6
outlining 53–4
overview 47

paragraphs 96
revised 61, 64–5
see also sentences

pattern of reports analysed
12, 14, 16
permanent report 98
personal pronouns 100
persuasion as purpose of
report 29–30, **94**
photocopying 43–4
pie charts 75–6, 79, 104
planning, *see* structure and
planning
pluralising sentences 100
point size of fonts 85–6, 87
preliminaries 97
introductions 13, 16, 96
preparation for research 37–8
presentation 7, 8, **82–9**
importance of 82–3
see also headings; space;
typeface
pressure group report 10,
14–15
printed resources 36, 41
process of writing 56–71
see also drafting; editing;
levels of writing; revision
pronouns 67, **100**
proposals, *see* executive
summary
proposition 48
publishing 73
purpose of report 27–31, 91–2,
94
information 27, **94**
interpretation 28
persuasion 29–30, **94**
as record 31, **94**

readability of typeface 86, 87
reader, *see* audience
recommendations, *see* executive summary
recording information 43–4
record as purpose of report
31, **94**
redrafting, *see* revision
remit/commission 32–3, **91–2**
reports 6–9

see also defining; editing;
      presentation; process;
      research; structure and
      planning; types
research and information
      sources **35–44**
   electronic 36, 42, 117–18
   human informants 36,
      38–40
   preparation for 37–8
   printed 36, 41
   recording and storing infor-
      mation 43–4
   working method 35–6
revision/rewriting
   and cutting 77–9
   of paragraphs 61, 64–5
   of sentences 61, 66–8
   of structure 61, 63
   of words 61, 68–71
   see also drafting
running head 89

sample reports 13, 15, **109–14**
   body and detail 15, 18–19
   brief formal **109–11**
   business committee 10,
      16-19, **111–15**
   conclusions 16, 19
   drafting 57–60
   editing 74, 75–6, 77–9
   layout 14
   see also types of report
scanning 44
script fonts 84
second draft 59
semi-formal style **93**
semi-informal style **93**
semi-permanent report **98**
sentences 64, 65, 101
   length 24, 25, 66, 67

revised 61, 66–8
   subject of 67–8
   see also paragraphs; words
sequential organisation 46,
      49, 74
serif and sans serif fonts 84–5
sexism, avoiding 100
short reports 50, **95**
   formal 10, 11–12, **109–11**
short sentences 67
short words 108
simplicity 50–1
size:
   of report, see length
   of type 85–6, 87
slang 99
space 82–3, 88, 89
status of report in remit 33
storing information 43–4
structure and planning **45–55**
   basic pattern 49
   detail versus simplicity 50–1
   editing 73–6
   process of planning 52–5
   revision 61, 63
   types of writing 45–8
   typical structures 49–50
style 7, 8, **93**
   see also formality; informality
subject of sentence 67–8
sub-sections, planning 52–3
summary, see executive
      summary

taboo words 99
teamwork 35–6, 80
technical words 24–5, 70–1
templates for reports **96–7**
temporary report **98**
terms of reference in remit 32
text fonts 82–3, 84

third draft 60
time:
   delaying final edit 81
   for reading reports 23
Times (font) 86
tone, see formality; informality
two-part reports 50
typeface (fonts) 82–6, 87, 89
   choosing 82–5
   readability 86, 87
   size 85
types of report **10–21**
   brief formal 10, 11–12,
      109–11
   business committee 10,
      16–19, **111–15**
   consumer research 10,
      13–14
   pressure group 10, 14–15
types of writing 45–8

underlining 87

verbs 108
   sentences without 101
visual presentation 27, 51,
      75–6, 79, 89, **102–8**
   see also charts

word processors, see computers
words:
   formal/informal 25, **99–100**
   long 24
   revised 61, 68–71
   see also paragraphs; sentences
workflow, see levels of writing
working method 35–6
writing, types of 45–8
   see also reports